ABC'S OF CREATIVE WRITING

David W. Booth / Stanley Skinner

Globe/Modern Curriculum Press
Toronto

Editor: Frank English
Designer: John Zehethofer

Printed and Bound in Canada
0 9 8 7 6 5 4 3

Canadian Cataloguing in Publication Data

Booth, David W., 1938-
    ABC's of creative writing

For use in schools.
Includes index.
ISBN 0-88996-048-8

1. English language - Rhetoric.   2. English
language - Composition and exercises.   I. Skinner,
Stanley.   II. Title.

PE1408.B66   808'.042   C81-094473-1

Acknowledgments

Every effort has been made to acknowledge all sources of material used in this book. The publishers would be grateful if any errors or omissions were pointed out, so that they may be corrected.

Acknowledgment is gratefully made for the use of the following copyright material:

"The Last Canoe" from *The Last Canoe* (1979) by John Craig. Reprinted by permission of Peter Martin Associates, Toronto. "Never Cry Wolf" from *Never Cry Wolf* (Copyright © 1963) by Farley Mowat. Reprinted by permission of Little, Brown and Company in association with the Atlantic Monthly Press, Boston and by permission of The Canadian Publishers, McClelland and Stewart Limited, Toronto. "Wild Cat" by Robert Newton Peck. Copyright © 1975 by Robert Newton Peck. Reprinted by permission of Holiday House, Inc., N.Y. "TV Exploits Nagging Power" by Mike Grenby (Copyright 1980 M&M Creations Ltd.) Reprinted by permission of M&M Creations Ltd., West Vancouver and *The Globe & Mail*, Toronto. "Geniesh" from *Geniesh* (1973) by Jane Willis. Reprinted by permission of General Publishing Limited, Don Mills, Ont. "My Genealogy" from *The Sad Truths* (1974) by John Robert Colombo. Reprinted by permission of the author. "Flavius Plourde" from *Alberta* by Robert Kroetsch. Copyright © Robert Kroetsch 1968. Reprinted by permission of Macmillan of Canada, a Division of Gage Publishing Limited, Agincourt, Ont. Jacket blurb of *The Planet of Junior Brown*, Copyright © 1971, by Virginia Hamilton. Reprinted by permission of Macmillan Publishing Co., Inc., N.Y., and *Saturday Review*, N.Y. Jacket blurb of *Hold Fast* by Kevin Major. © 1978 by Kevin Major. Used by permission of Clarke, Irwin & Company Limited, Toronto. "Hockey Fever in Goganne Falls" from *Hockey Fever in Goganne Falls* by R. J. Childerhose. Reprinted by permission of Macmillan of Canada, a Division of Gage Publishing Limited, Agincourt, Ont. "Landscape Poem" by Dom Sylvester Houedard from *20th Century Poetry and Poetics* © by the poet. Reprinted by permission of Ceolfrith Press, Sunderland, England. "Recipe for Eats Poems" from *Eats* by Arnold Adoff. Copyright © 1979 by Arnold Adoff. By permission of Lothrop, Lee & Shepard (A Division of William Morrow & Company). "Dedication" from *Cats, Cats, Cats, Cats, Cats* by Beatrice Schenk de Regniers, published by Pantheon Books. Reprinted by permission of the author. "What Is a Hamburger?" and "What Are Mim People?" from *Ounce, Dice, Trice* by Alastair Reid. Copyright © 1958 by Alastair Reid and Ben Shahn. By permission of Little, Brown and Company in association with the Atlantic Monthly Press. "An Indian Summer Day on the prairie" from *Collected Poems* by Vachel Lindsay. Reprinted by permission of Macmillan Publishing Co., Inc. Copyright 1914 by Macmillan Publishing Co., Inc., renewed 1942 by Elizabeth C. Lindsay. "Kayak Song in Dialogue" — Ammassalik Eskimo. Reprinted with permission of The Macmillan Publishing Co., Inc. from *The Unwritten Song*, Vol. 1, edited and with translations by Willard R. Trask. Copyright © 1966 by Willard R. Trask. "Diary of a Homesteader" from *Grass Roots* by Heather Robertson. Reprinted by permission of James Lorimer, Publisher, Toronto. "The Diary of Trilby Frost" by Dianne Glaser. Copyright © 1976 by Dianne Glaser. Reprinted from *The Diary of Trilby Frost* by permission of Holiday House, Inc., N.Y. "4:30 a.m., Monday, 21 October 1805" from *Monday, 21 October 1805* by Ian Ribbons, © Ian Ribbons 1968. Reprinted by permission of Oxford University Press, England. "The Coming of the Plague" from *Collected Poems* by Weldon Kees, by permission of University of Nebraska Press. "A Southern Saskatchewan Farmer's Wife" from *The Canadian Inventions Book* by Janis Nostbakken and Jack Humphreys. Reprinted with the permission of the publisher, Greey de Pencier Books, Toronto. "Bullets in the Bush" reprinted by permission of *The Globe and Mail*, Toronto. "John James Hume, Esq." from *Early Ontario Gravestones* by Carole Hanks. Copyright © McGraw-Hill Ryerson Limited, 1974. Reprinted by permission. "Uncles" excerpted from *Guy Lenny* by Harry Mazer.

Copyright © 1971 by Harry Mazer. Reprinted by permission of Delacorte Press, N.Y. "Subway" from *By Camel and by Car* by Guy Billout. © 1979 by Guy Billout Published by Prentice-Hall, Inc., Englewood Cliffs, N.J. "Remembrance of Letter Writing" by Anthony Prete. Reprinted with permission from the Dec. 1979 issue of *Media & Methods* magazine. © 1979, North American Publishing Company. "Eulogy for Jesse James" from the film "Jesse James" — Twentieth Century-Fox (1939). By permission. "How Birds Fly" from *The Penguin Book of the Natural World*. Reprinted by permission of Penguin Books Ltd., England. "How to Tell a Tornado" by Howard Mohr from *Minnesota English Journal*, Vol. IX, Fall 1973. Reprinted by permission. "The Glass in the Field" by James Thurber. Copyright © 1940 James Thurber. Copyright © 1968 Helen W. Thurber. From *Fables for Our Time* published by Harper & Row, N.Y. "The Princess and the Peas" from *The Classic Fairy Tales* by Iona and Peter Opie, © Iona and Peter Opie 1974. Reprinted by permission of Oxford University Press, England. "Rapunzel, Rapunzel" from *Good Morning* by Mark Van Doren. Reprinted by permission of Farrar, Straus & Giroux, Inc., N.Y. "The Horse that had a Flat Tire" from *The Pill Versus the Springhill Mine Disaster* by Richard Brautigan. Copyright © 1968 by Richard Brautigan. Reprinted by permission of Delacorte Press/Seymour Lawrence, N.Y. "The Zoo in Your Dreams" from *Chance, Luck and Destiny* by Peter Dickinson. Reprinted by permission of Victor Gollancz Ltd., and Little, Brown and Company in association with The Atlantic Monthly Press. "Spells" from *The Wandering Man* by James Reeves. Reprinted by permission of William Heinemann Ltd., England. "The Old Men Admiring Themselves in the Water" from *Collected Poems of W. B. Yeats*. Reprinted by permission of M. B. Yeats, Anne Yeats, Macmillan London Limited, and The Macmillan Publishing Co., Inc., N.Y. "Ice Cream Cone" from *Pop Poems* by Ronald Gross. Copyright © 1967 by Ronald Gross. Reprinted by permission of Simon & Schuster, a Division of Gulf & Western Corporation. "Grizzly at Night" from *The Ghosts Call You Poor* by Andrew Suknaski. © Andrew Suknaski 1978. Reprinted by permission of Macmillan of Canada, a Division of Gage Publishing Limited, Agincourt, Ont. "The Projectionist's Nightmare" from *Notes to the Hurrying Man* by Brian Patten. Reprinted by permission of Farrar, Straus & Giroux, Inc., N.Y. "The Werewolf" from *Nightmares* by Jack Prelutsky. Copyright © 1976 by Jack Prelutsky. By permission of Greenwillow Books (a Division of William Morrow & Company). "The Thing in the Cellar" by David H. Keller. Reprinted by permission of Arkham House Publishers, Inc., Wisconsin. Haiku poems. Translations from *Haiku* Vols. 1-4 by R. H. Blyth. Copyright © 1945-52 R. H. Blyth, reprinted by permission of The Hokuseido Press, Tokyo. "Hymn to the Sun" by Akhenaton, translated by Manchip White. Reprinted by permission of Dover Books, N.Y. "James Houston" by Phil Surguy (1980). Reprinted by permission of Books in Canada. "The Death of Evening Star" excerpt from *The Death of Evening Star* by Leonard Everett Fisher. Copyright © 1972 by Leonard Everett Fisher. Reprinted by permission of Doubleday & Company, Inc., N.Y. "Hark, Hark, the Dogs Do Bark" from *The Inner City Mother Goose* by Eve Merriam. Copyright for text © Eve Merriam. Reprinted by permission of the author. Graphics by Lawrence Ratzkin, by permission of Marvin Josephson Associates. "The Sky Has Fallen" from *Zuni Mythology* by Ruth Benedict (1935). Reprinted by permission Columbia University Press, N.Y. "Merlin and the Snake's Egg" from *Merlin and the Snake's Egg* by Leslie Norris. Copyright © 1978 by Leslie Norris. Reprinted by permission of Viking Penguin Inc., N.Y. "Miss Kelly" from *Soup* by Robert Newton Peck. Copyright © by Robert Newton Peck. Reprinted by permission of Alfred A. Knopf, Inc., N.Y. "Last Letter" from *Translations from the English* (Toronto, 1974) by John Robert Colombo. Reprinted by permission of the author. "Vic Dardick" from Peter Gzowski's *Book About This Country in the Morning*. Reprinted by permission of Hurtig Publishers, Edmonton. "And My Heart Soars" by Chief Dan George.

(continued on page 154)

Contents

What Is Writing?

Every day you read the words that other people have written — advertisements, posters, record covers, letters, magazines, and books. Behind everything you read is a writer. Writers have many reasons for writing: they might wish to express personal thoughts in a diary or a journal; they might wish to communicate a message to a friend something they feel needs to be said; or they might intend their work to be published and, therefore, treat their writing as an art form to be polished and perfected.

Through the act of writing, you can examine and make sense of your experiences and think creatively about them. Sometimes your writing will be private; other times you will want someone to read your work. If you wish to write effectively, you must believe that you have something to say that is of value, and that what you write will be of interest to others.

Patterns for Writing

Reading what other people have written often triggers ideas for your own writing. For example, if you were to read a poem entitled ''The Dinner Table'' you might recall a similar incident in your own life. The associations and images created in your mind can then be used as the basis for a new composition. Your piece of writing may have a theme different from the original that would set off its own reactions in the next reader's mind.

As a writer, you will use specific patterns to help you express ideas and feelings. You have already experienced many of these patterns in your life: poems, novels, songs, and scripts. You as a writer will choose the pattern that best suits your purpose. For example, should you wish to express your feelings about love, you do not need to write a Valentine verse. Instead, you might choose the pattern of an invitation, a prayer, or a list. These patterns provide writing structures that you can use to order and arrange your ideas.

A Writing Program

Writing is a process that consists of three stages: pre-writing, writing, and post-writing.

Pre-writing is the stage at which you think about some of the general issues and begin to find your own particular viewpoint. Discussion with other students will help you clarify your thoughts and perceptions, develop a focus, and organize your information. As well, pre-writing includes jotting down notes, research, making summaries, and outlining.

The second stage of the process *is the writing* of the first draft of the composition, a step on the way to the finished product. When you re-read this draft, you should hear its message and see the shape of the literary pattern emerging.

This draft is your first written expression of what you wish to say and how you wish to say it. Your composition will alter as you elaborate and expand upon your ideas.

At this time, you must be aware of the impact your composition will have on the listener or reader. By reading this draft to other students and by listening to their responses, you will learn whether you have communicated your thoughts successfully. Therefore, your composition will have to be well-organized, accurate, complete, and interesting.

Post-writing is the editing and revising stage. The process of editing also includes the examination of the structure and mechanics of your composition. The structure must be appropriate and effective; it includes the pattern, the language, the sentences, and the word choice. Mechanics concern spelling, punctuation, capitalization, and handwriting. Although secondary to the message, the mechanics of writing are essential to clear communication. As you edit, you should revise the structure and the mechanics where necessary.

Once finished, your writing can then be shared with a teacher, other students, the whole class, the rest of the school, parents, and outsiders. It may be read aloud, published in a class newspaper, or in the school yearbook. You will be writing for a real purpose.

How to Use This Book

This book is intended to help you develop as a writer. It contains a selection of writing patterns that will help you express your own ideas and feelings. By using the writings of others as a starting point, you will be able to choose and experiment with different forms of expression, using a variety of patterns.

The book is arranged alphabetically by pattern. Each pattern contains a brief description of the pattern, literary selections, and a series of activities.

Through the activities, you will explore themes and issues and experiment with literary patterns. The Cross-reference Index at the back of the book will allow you to use the patterns in a variety of ways.

Please note: 1) that each author's own style of spelling and punctuation has been retained; 2) that measurement is in metric units except where a poet has used other units.

A writing checklist

Pre-writing:
general discussion
brainstorming of ideas
clarification of the issues
jotting down notes
developing a focus
choosing a meaningful topic
researching facts
organizing information
summarizing the information
creating an outline

Writing:
writing a first draft
expanding ideas
elaborating points
verifying grammar through
    textbook
considering the audience
re-reading the draft
reading the draft aloud to
    other students

Post-writing:
editing the ideas
revising the structure and the content
proofreading for mechanics
checking spelling through dictionary
sharing with others
publishing

Adventure stories are concerned with action and excitement. As you read, you seem to experience the events as they happen. The plot draws you on — you want to keep reading. The adventure absorbs you.

The Last Canoe

For the first few days, it didn't seem like anything special or very different to Arthur. He knew that each paddle-stroke was taking him farther away from Sarah and the rest of what had been his life, but in the beginning the country looked familiar, much like his own.

A lot of it was still forest, with, here and there, patchwork farms, seldom prosperous looking, for the soil was thin and grudging, little more than a dusting of sand between the quartz and granite outcroppings of the Great Shield. Piles of stones in the fields. Split-cedar rail fences. A few black-and-white pasturing cows.

• • •

Now and then someone waved to him — a young woman poised on a diving board, a man still fishing from an old, white skiff or a party of tourists looking down from a steel bridge. But although there were plenty of people around, Arthur felt no desire for company or talk, not when he would, so soon, be truly alone.

The numerous locks slowed him down, as he had known they would. He portaged around some, waited at others to lock through with other, larger craft. But in spite of the obstacles, he was putting ten or twelve kilometres a day behind his paddle. When night fell, he made camp wherever he could find an unoccupied point or small island, sleeping under the tarpaulin or under the overturned canoe when it rained.

At the end of the third day he reached the weedy bay from which the Trent River begins its journey south to Lake Ontario. That evening, in the lingering July twilight, he made the first entry in his diary.

July 3:
Well, pretty good so far. Had a few aches, but mostly better now. Caught a 'lunge this afternoon (pretty little!) and had it for supper. This is the easy part, I guess, along here. Wonder how things are back home? Don't suppose I'll get much rest.

After another three days, he had finished with the Trent and made a good beginning on his long journey to the east.

July 6:
Started out into the big lake this afternoon. Not as bad as I expected. They call this the Bay of Quinte. The shore comes pretty close on both sides, and there isn't much wind. A man on a big boat told me that it will be like this most of the way to Kingston. Only a couple of open stretches to worry about. That's good!

But Lake Ontario was not prepared to let him slip by so unmarked.

July 8:
Luck bad. Real strong east wind yesterday and to-day. Hard paddling in big swells. Just about swamped four or five times. Had to get down on bottom and let her drift. Got washed up on shore just before dark. Canoe and me all right but plenty wet. Think I'm on Amherst Island.

July 9:
Been here all day. Have never seen waves like it — some a lot taller than me. Not the ocean yet, though. There's a glow over east that must be Kingston. Don't know when I'll be able to get over there. Had some pemmican tonight. Just have to wait — that's all I can do.

JOHN CRAIG

1 What makes this selection an adventure story?

2 This selection is Chapter 7 in the book. What has gone before? Write the opening chapter, in which you introduce Arthur and send him on his mission.

3 Write a diary entry of Arthur's first view of the Atlantic — the ocean that he must cross alone.

4 You are a reporter watching Arthur leave on his mission. Tell your readers your impression of him and his mission.

Advertisements

Advertisements are written to persuade; that is, they help sell something to someone. They may deal with a service or a product. Advertisements incorporate both words and pictures.

1 What is each of these advertisements selling?
2 Write an advertisement in which Alexander Graham Bell discusses his invention, the telephone.
3 Using the technique of a story within an advertisement, create an advertisement for a hand-held hairdryer.
4 A common technique used in advertisements is endorsement by famous people. Write an essay in which a sports heroine says why she refuses to endorse products.

A TREE IS GOD'S CREATION. TO THE ARTIST INSPIRATION, TO THE HOMEOWNER SHELTER, BEAUTY, TO MOTHER NATURE A WILDLIFE HOME, TO ALL...MAN'S EVER USEFUL, EVERLASTING FRIEND

TREES...A GROWING CONCERN

CANADIAN FORESTRY ASSOCIATION AND YOUR PROVINCIAL FORESTRY ASSOCIATION

Who says Edison's greatest invention wasn't the light bulb?
Thomas Edison.

"Some people have called the light bulb my greatest invention. I'd have to disagree.

It wasn't the light bulb. Or the phonograph. Or the motion picture. I think my greatest invention was the commercial research lab. A place where I could develop all kinds of inventions.

I built the very first commercial research lab in the country in Menlo Park, New Jersey, in 1876.

You could say that was the start of the General Electric Company. But, of course, I didn't know it at the time.

At Menlo Park, we had as many as 44 different inventions under way at the same time. Sometimes you couldn't hear yourself think. Of course, in my case it didn't matter. I've been deaf since I was twelve.

It was my goal to turn out a minor invention every ten days and a big thing every six months or so.

Two of my big things were the light bulb and the power plant. They had to be developed at the same time. Because I had no hope of selling the light bulb if there was no electricity. And I had no hope of selling electricity unless there was a light bulb.

The company I set up to sell the light bulb was called the Edison Electric Light Company. Later, it became the General Electric Company.

How did I get in the whole inventing business anyway?

Quite frankly, I saw it as a way to make some money. When I was a newsboy, I had a chance to learn that money can be made out of a little careful thought. And, being poor, I already knew that money was a valuable thing.

Boys who don't know that are under a disadvantage greater than deafness."

 The research tradition Thomas Edison started continues today at the General Electric Research and Development Center in Schenectady, N.Y. Over the years, this General Electric laboratory has pioneered many developments such as the x-ray, industrial plastics, radio, television, the jet engine, Man-Made™ diamonds.

Progress for People.
GENERAL ⊕ ELECTRIC

Animal stories

Animal stories can be real or fictional. They concern humans interacting with animals, or animals as observed by humans, or animals having human qualities. The story can be told either from the viewpoint of the animal or the human.

Never Cry Wolf

I decided to pitch my tent on a gravel ridge above the cabin, and here I was vainly trying to go to sleep that evening when I became aware of unfamiliar sounds. Sitting bolt upright, I listened intently.

The sounds were coming from just across the river, to the north, and they were a weird medley of whines, whimpers and small howls. My grip on the rifle slowly relaxed. If there is one thing at which scientists are adept, it is learning from experience; I was not to be fooled twice. The cries were obviously those of a Husky, probably a young one, and I deducted that it must be one of Mike's dogs (he owned three half-grown pups not yet trained to harness which ran loose after the team) that had got lost, retraced its way to the cabin, and was now begging for someone to come and be nice to it.

I was delighted. If that pup needed a friend, a chum, I was its man! I climbed hastily into my clothes, ran down to the riverbank, launched the canoe, and paddled lustily for the far bank.

The pup had never ceased its mournful plaint, and I was about to call out reassuringly when it occurred to me that an unfamiliar human voice might frighten it. I decided to stalk it instead, and to betray my presence only when I was close enough for soothing murmurs.

From the nature of the sounds I had assumed the dog was only a few yards away from the far bank, but as I made my way in the dim half-light, over broken boulders and across gravel ridges, the sounds seemed to remain at the same volume while I appeared to be getting no closer. I assumed the pup was retreating, perhaps out of shyness. In my anxiety not to startle it away entirely, I still kept quiet, even when the whimpering wail stopped, leaving me uncertain about the right direction to pursue. However, I saw a steep ridge looming ahead of me and I suspected that, once I gained its summit, I would have a clear enough view to enable me to locate the lost animal. As I neared the crest of the ridge I got down on my stomach (practicing the fieldcraft I had learned in the Boy Scouts) and cautiously inched my way the last few feet.

My head came slowly over the crest — and there was my quarry. He was lying down, evidently resting after his mournful singsong, and his nose was about six feet from mine. We stared at one another in silence. I do not know what went on in his massive skull, but my head was full of the most disturbing thoughts. I was peering straight into the amber gaze of a fully grown arctic wolf, who probably weighed more than I did, and who was certainly a lot better versed in close-combat techniques than I would ever be.

For some seconds neither of us moved but continued to stare hypnotically into one another's eyes. The wolf was the first to break the spell. With a spring which would have done justice to a Russian dancer, he leaped about a metre straight into the air and came down running. The textbooks say a wolf can run thirty kilometres an hour, but this one did not appear to be running, so much as flying low. Within seconds he had vanished from my sight.

FARLEY MOWAT

Wild Cat

The calico kitten was now six weeks old.

For the past few days, she had still tried to suck milk, but her mother was drying up and cuffed her away. It was time she was weaned. Better food lay in wait for her. Meat. A passing mouse had once given her hunger.

Several times a day, the two cats would leave their den between the two buildings to hunt. Each trip began and ended with a stop behind the diner where the teamsters ate. Another building nearby had long since been abandoned by rent-paying tenants. But several families lived there; without heat, without water, and without glass in any of the windows. They threw the remains of a meal out of a smashed window and into the street or the alley. An old lady tossed scrapings from a can of tuna to the cats. As she tried to pet them, they darted away.

It was dark. And along this new alley, near the damp wall of the condemned tenement, the mother cat and her calico kitten walked. The older cat held her ears up, locked as always into a position of constant alert. The least noise made her turn her head; and since the streets of the center city were rife with noise, her head constantly moved, even while she ate.

An hour later, it started to rain. The cat sought shelter, but the kitten held her face into the wet wind, letting it wash her clean. She had never been wet before. It was cold and shocking, yet somehow welcome. Her body fought the rain with a pleasant internal tingle that made her aware of thirst. Opening her tiny mouth, she gulped a raindrop. Drop by drop, she swallowed the water from the sky.

Hunching down side by side in the darkness, the two cats waited out the rainstorm. It lasted for three hours, and yet they did not move. As the rain finally ended, the kitten heard a slight noise in the corner of the blackness. There! There it was again. Opening her green eyes wide, she strained to see what was in the dark that made the noise.

A small gray mouse moved under an empty cigarette pack. His hole was now flooded, and so to keep his tiny feet dry, he moved upward out of his hiding place, pushing the paper pack with his shoulders. The transparent wrapping crackled as he moved. And just as he moved again, the calico kitten's paws hammered down on him and pinned him to the earth.

The kitten had never caught a mouse before. This was the first, and as it wiggled under her claws, she pushed down hard with all her weight. Out he squirmed. But she was too quick for him. As her body shot forward, her small teeth closed on his head. He fought with all his strength to be free of her, kicking his small body against her lips. But with a sudden hitch of her head and a second snap of her jaws, she caught more of him, breaking his spine as her teeth closed once again.

She liked the taste. His flesh was warm like the milk of her mother, though better. She was a hunter and in her mouth was the sweet flavor of a kill.

But the mouse was torn away from her. The mother cat was hungry too. So hungry that she wanted the mouse for herself. The mother sprung at it when the kitten's jaws relaxed for an instant. The fight for the mouse was brief. As the kitten sprang again at the mouse which was now in her mother's mouth, the bigger cat swatted her back. From deep in her mother's throat came a sound that the kitten had never heard, a threatening growl. Its meaning was clear.

But yet the kitten tried once more to claim her kill — until stronger claws raked across her nose, drawing blood and making her sick with pain.

Out from under the tenement stairs she fled. The night was still cold and wet. Once more she heard the warning from her mother's throat, as she looked back. It was the last time she ever saw her mother.

But now she was no longer a kitten who would mew in the dark. Although afraid, she would never again seek her mother's warm silky side.

ROBERT NEWTON PECK

1 In what categories of animal story do these two selections fall?

2 You are the wolf. Describe your meeting with this human.

3 You are the cat's parents. Describe what you saw.

4 This alley cat lives only one more year. Write her epitaph.

Announcements

An announcement is a public declaration of an event that has happened or should happen. The announcement is usually expressed in formal language and is issued by someone in authority.

An Announcement

This is your last warning!
If you continue to ignore me,
If you continue to show no interest
in learning my name,
If you have not spoken a phrase of some sort to
    me
by the end of next week —
I will stop dreaming about you.
The Great American Novel
now being formulated in my head,
of which you are the central character,
will be terminated!
I've given you ample, fair, silent warning.
I await your actions.

MARY LONG

For Sale

One sister for sale!
One sister for sale!
One crying and spying young sister for sale!
I'm really not kidding,
So who'll start the bidding?
Do I hear a dollar?
A nickel?
A penny?
Oh, isn't there, isn't there, isn't there any
One kid who will buy this old sister for sale,
This crying and spying young sister for sale?

SHEL SILVERSTEIN

1 To whom are these announcements made?

2 What led up to this auctioning announcement? Write the breakfast scene that caused this announcement to be given.

3 Using the pattern of "An Announcement," write a poem expressing your concern about your frustrations.

4 Supposing that you have found out that someone is writing a book about you. Write the announcement that you would send to the author, warning him or her that your life is private.

Article

An article is a type of essay found in a newspaper or magazine. It is self-contained and treats one subject in an informative manner. Its purpose is both to educate and to entertain.

TV exploits nagging power

Television advertisers certainly know what they are doing when they aim their commercials at children. Children rarely have money, but they do have nagging power.

All the advertiser has to do is convince the child he or she should have something, and then the child pressures the parent to buy it.

How, then, do you explain to a child who typically watches some 20 000 television commercials a year that you don't want or simply cannot afford to buy what those ads are pushing?

Telling a 4-year-old that "we can't afford" a particular toy is meaningless because the child probably has no idea where the family's income originates, or that spending is limited by that income. And slightly older children are likely to reply: "Just write a cheque, Mum," or "Use a credit card if you don't have any money."

The average pre-schooler watches 25 to 30 hours of TV a week. Even after the child starts school, he or she still watches about 20 to 25 hours. That adds up to considerable "I want" and "Let's buy" pressure on parents.

"Even at fairly advanced stages, children don't understand about money and commerce," says Tannis MacBeth Williams, a University of B.C. psychology professor who directed a major study on how TV affects people, children in particular.

"Young children don't realize that commercials are aimed at selling products and services, at making money for the sponsors. The children think advertisers like them and are showing them toys and candy because these are the things children should have.

"The child is then confused when a parent objects to buying these items. And the child is further confused if the parent tries to explain that the family can't afford a particular toy, for example.

"Parent and child simply aren't communicating because the child doesn't understand what 'afford' means."

Professor Williams cited U.S. psychologist Hans Furth, whose research has shown that at the earliest stage, children believe the source of their parents' income is the change they receive at the store.

At another stage, children believe money comes from the government. As development proceeds, they eventually come to understand how and why shopkeepers buy goods and resell them to customers at a higher price.

It also takes a while before children understand the purpose and techniques of advertising. And until they learn all this information, it is very difficult for parents to deal with the "I want" effect of TV commercials.

"There is not much point in explaining to the average 4-year-old that the family cannot afford something the child has seen advertised on TV if the child is incapable of understanding about money," Prof. Williams said.

"Simply talking and teaching and trying to explain won't help. The child has to live and learn through experience before he or she can understand certain concepts like family income and basic commerce."

Prof. Williams said people often forget that TV was originally developed in the United States to make money, not primarily to entertain or educate. "So you always come back to the problem when you deal with something like the effects of commercials on children."

What can a parent do to counter or at least minimize the negative effects of TV commercials on children? Prof. Williams suggested the following:

☐ Have a talk with your child to find out just how much he or she understands about commercials ("Why do they show you pictures of fast food/toys/candy on TV?") and about money ("Where do we get our money to go shopping?"). The child's answers will enable you to discuss both commercials and money on a level the child can understand.

☐ Watch TV with your child and discuss what he or she sees. "Oh, they are just trying to get us to go to McDonald's by showing us those pictures," you might say. If the child understands something about money, you could then add: "When we go to McDonald's, we have to pay our money to the people who own McDonald's."

If there has just been an ad for sugar-coated cereals, for example, you could point out: "So much sugar is bad for you and makes holes on your teeth, so we don't buy those sorts of cereals" — presuming that indeed is your family's policy. Or if the ad is for a poorly made toy, you could say: "It looks like a good toy, but it breaks very quickly."

As well as countering bad ads, reinforce the good ones, the public service ads about the importance of exercising or brushing teeth, for example.

☐ If the idea of watching 25 hours of TV a week with your child turns you off, then turn off the TV more often. And whenever possible, restrict the selection to PBS, the no-ad public TV network, and to CBC, which has no ads on programs aimed at children under 12.

☐ Encourage consumer education in the schools to help children understand about the basics of commerce and money management.

MIKE GRENBY

1 Summarize this article in 25 words.

2 Choose one of the suggestions presented by the writer. Imagine the discussion that would occur in your family, then write the transcript.

3 You are the father of a six-year-old who has written to Santa Claus asking for a specific toy advertised on TV. As Santa Claus, write a letter to your child explaining why he or she will not get the toy for Christmas.

4 Write an article expressing your point of view on the issue of film classification.

Autobiography

An autobiography is the story of one's own life. The author looks back on his or her life, selects certain important incidents, and weaves a story around them.

Geniesh

"Oh, there's the house," my mother said, pointing at a tarpaper-covered shack. She must have seen the look of dismay on my face because she added, "The outside isn't finished yet."

I walked in expectantly, but I was appalled at the shabbiness and seediness that surrounded me. Had I, for fifteen years, lived amid such utter poverty? Had I become a snob — as my friends had predicted I would — looking down at my own people and their old ways? My outlook and my feelings, I told myself, could not have changed so drastically in a few years.

The two-room shack was clean, but placed against a city slum, the slum would look like a palace. Against one ill-fitted, beaverboard wall was a heavily gouged wooden table loaded with an assortment of cracked and chipped porcelain. Around the table was an odd mixture of seats: one wooden chair with a missing back, a wooden bench as heavily gouged as the table, a large piece of tree trunk, and the old fold-away bed, which was always left unfolded and which collapsed when some unsuspecting visitor sat too close to either end.

Against the opposite wall sat an old wood-stove with an oven door that would not close. Against this stove was the ninety-litre water container into which everybody dipped their cups as they needed a drink. Beside it sat a forty-litre slop pail full of dirty dish water, tea leaves, coffee grounds, and bones. Right next to it was a soap-scummed wash stand with a badly chipped white porcelain basin in it. There were no other furnishings in the front room.

The back room was jammed with three wooden beds of varying sizes, one broken-down dresser, an old steamship trunk, and cardboard boxes filled with clothes and other belongings. Draped over the clotheslines that criss-crossed the room were clean, ironed clothes. Six people — my three sisters, my brother, my mother, and my stepfather — slept in this room.

"You can sleep on this bed," my mother said, pointing to the fold-away bed in the front room. "It's the only one with a mattress."

When she suggested I eat, I told her I wanted to see my grandmother first. Actually, I wanted to get away for a while, to try and regain my perspective.

"How can they live like that?" I asked myself repeatedly. Yet, I could not deny the fact that they were completely happy even though they lacked what I had come to consider the essentials of life — electricity, indoor plumbing, all the comforts of modern living. I realized that a person could have all these things and still be unhappy. Love and happiness were all that mattered.

JANE WILLIS

My Genealogy

1.
My great-great-grandfather
played in the streets
of Milano, I am told.
I take it on faith.

2.
His son, the artisan,
immigrated to Baden, Ontario,
as a decorator or builder.
I believe this, but never met him.

3.
My grandfather was born
in Baden, and he married
a German girl there.
I remember him well —
he spoke English
with a German accent.

4.
My grandparents lived
in Berlin, Ontario,
when it changed its name
to honour Lord Kitchener.
They made an unusual couple —
he was more than six feet tall,
she barely five — but together
they produced fourteen children.

5.
One of these fourteen Colombos
was my father. He spoke English
with a Pennsylvania-Dutch accent.

6.
He married a Kitchener girl,
and I was born in that city —
with its light industry
and its farmer's market —
in that city, an only child.

7.
I remember quite distinctly
my mother's parents, my grandparents. My grandfather spoke
with a thick Greek accent,
and my larger grandmother,
a nasal Quebec French. Yes,
they made a colourful couple.

8.
They first met in Montreal,
lived in Toronto for a while,
finally settled in Kitchener.
They had five children,
and their arguments had to be
heard to be believed.

9.
Blood flows through my veins
at different speeds:
Italian, German,
Greek, French-Canadian.
Sometimes it mixes.

10.
At times I feel close
to the Aegean,
the Côte d'Azure,
the Lombard Plain,
and the Black Forest.

11.
I seldom feel close
to the Rocky Mountains,
the Prairies,
the Great Lakes,
or the cold St. Lawrence.
What am I doing in Toronto?

12.
If this means being a Canadian,
I am a Canadian.

JOHN ROBERT COLOMBO

1 Discuss these authors' impressions of the past.

2 *Geniesh* is an emotional description of a woman's life. In this selection, she describes her home as a shack. Using the style of stream of consciousness, describe her feelings.

3 Write your ''genealogy,'' real or imaginary, based on this model.

4 Write a mini-biography, based on your life, but written as if by another person.

Ballad

A ballad is a poem that can be sung or recited, telling a story in a simple but dramatic way. In the past, ballads were passed from generation to generation orally, helping people to remember their history. Since then, poets and singers have used the traditional ballad form to create "literary" ballads.

Jesse James

It was on a Wednesday night, the moon was
   shining bright,
    They robbed the Glendale train.
And the people they did say, from near and far,
    'Twas the outlaws Frank and Jesse James.

Refrain:
   Jesse had a wife to mourn all her life,
     The children they are brave.
   'Twas a dirty little coward shot Mister Howard,
     And laid Jesse James in his grave.

It was Robert Ford, the dirty little coward,
   I wonder how he does feel,
For he ate of Jesse's bread and he slept in Jesse's
   bed,
    Then he laid Jesse James in his grave.

Refrain

It was his brother Frank that robbed the Gallatin
   bank,
    And carried the money from the town.
It was in this very place that they had a little
   race,
    For they shot Captain Sheets to the ground.

Refrain

They went to the crossing not very far from
   there,
    And there they did the same;
And the agent on his knees he delivered up the
   keys
    To the outlaws Frank and Jesse James.

Refrain

It was on a Saturday night, Jesse was at home
   Talking to his family brave,
When the thief and the coward, little Robert
   Ford,
    Laid Jesse James in his grave.

Refrain

How people held their breath when they heard
   of Jesse's death,
    And wondered how he ever came to die
'Twas one of the gang, dirty Robert Ford,
    That shot Jesse James on the sly.

Refrain

Jesse went to his rest with his hand on his
   breast.
    The devil will be upon his knee.
He was born one day in the county of Clay,
    And came from a solitary race.

Refrain

ANONYMOUS

Annabel Lee

It was many and many a year ago,
   In a kingdom by the sea,
That a maiden there lived whom you may know
   By the name of Annabel Lee;
And this maiden she lived with no other thought
   Than to love and be loved by me.

I was a child and *she* was a child,
   In this kingdom by the sea,
But we loved with a love that was more than
   love —
   I and my Annabel Lee —
With a love that the wingèd seraphs of Heaven
   Coveted her and me.

And this was the reason that, long ago,
    In this kingdom by the sea,
A wind blew out of a cloud, chilling
    My beautiful Annabel Lee;
So that her highborn kinsmen came
    And bore her away from me,
To shut her up in a sepulcher
    In this kingdom by the sea.

The angels, not half so happy in Heaven,
    Went envying her and me: —
Yes! — that was the reason (as all men know,
    In this kingdom by the sea)
That the wind came out of the cloud by night,
    Chilling and killing my Annabel Lee.

But our love it was stronger by far than the love
    Of those who were older than we —
    Of many far wiser than we —
And neither the angels in Heaven above,
    Nor the demons down under the sea,
Can ever dissever my soul from the soul
    Of the beautiful Annabel Lee: —

For the moon never beams, without bringing me dreams
    Of the beautiful Annabel Lee;
And the stars never rise, but I feel the bright eyes
    Of the beautiful Annabel Lee:
And so, all the night-tide, I lie down by the side
Of my darling — my darling — my life and my bride,
    In the sepulcher there by the sea —
    In her tomb by the sounding sea.

EDGAR ALLAN POE

1 How do these two ballads differ?

2 Rewrite the ballad "Jesse James" as if you were Jesse James or his wife. Base your ballad directly on the words and rhythm of the selection here.

3 Rewrite the ballad "Annabel Lee" in the third person, as if you were a storyteller.

4 You are either Jesse James or Annabel Lee. At the anniversary of your death, your ghost returns to haunt the place where you died. Create the monologue you speak on that occasion.

Biography

A biography is a description of a person's life. It is written by someone who either knew the person or who researched the facts in that person's life. The purpose of a biography is to transform the events in a person's life into an informative and interesting story.

Flavius Plourde

Flavius Plourde is eighty-three years old — 'I'm pretty near an old man now,' he said, laughing, his face free of wrinkles and almost beatific in its radiant good humour. He invited me into the modest house where he has lived alone since the death of his wife.

He was married in 1908 to a girl from the Gaspé; he himself was then living in Dame-Du-Lac on Lac Temiscouata, Quebec, and he worked first as a sportsmen's guide in the hunting-country around the lake. But he had a fever to be off and wandering, and the young couple went to Rhode Island.

By 1912 they were travelling west to the fabled Peace River country with a group of fellow *Canadiens* who were leaving the States and the mills for the promise of new land and a freer life. The Plourdes travelled the old route into the country: a trip that began in earnest at Athabasca Landing. The winter ride from there to Grouard lasted three and a half days, if you had an excellent team.

M. Plourde was modest about his excellent command of English. As a result we struck on a delightful way of communicating: we looked at his lifetime collection of photographs and snapshots.

He led me to the old buffet in his dining-room. On the dining-room table were a collection of fossils and rocks he has picked up in this region, and a bouquet of flowers made of foam rubber by a little niece. He explained that he and his wife had no children. The first pictures were of cousins: one family with eight daughters, another with two priests to its credit. He showed me two photographs of the big old house in which he was born in Quebec, a house much larger than any I have seen in the Peace River country. He showed me a picture of his father's sawmill, then of his father: a photograph taken one hundred years ago, the father stiff and lean and young behind a magnificent beard.

Flavius Plourde was a very handsome young guide with a dark moustache, and women obviously delighted in being photographed with him. He has pictures of a beautiful woman sharing a canoe he built, others of a very stout dowager from Philadelphia who shot a moose and posed with Flavius and the antlers. He has pictures of himself calling moose, with Sugarloaf Mountain in the background, more of a hunting-lodge.

Then he brought out a large and carefully posed photograph of a group of men and women standing beside a train in Duluth, Minnesota. 'Which is me?' he challenged, laughing. Flavius Plourde stood young and confident beside his young wife, in a group of pioneers who were leaving Rhode Island and Massachusetts for new homes in the wilderness.

The next picture was of only a few of those men, sitting on the bow of a river-steamer. Flavius counted — only he and one other man were now surviving. But the exploits of each were fresh in his mind: that man became mayor, that man went on to British Columbia, that man was pinned under a truck at 5 p.m. and was found dying the next morning at nine.

M. Plourde homesteaded five kilometres north of Falher. The country was mostly bush, with a little prairie. He used an axe and a plough and oxen, and he has snapshots of his homestead shack with four people standing proudly in a row before its low door; he has a picture of his log barn, of the first calf born on his homestead.

'Gee whiz,' he said, for we had hardly begun, 'I got lots of pictures.'

ROBERT KROETSCH

1 If there are many pioneers still left in Alberta, why did the author choose to write about Flavius Plourde?

2 Write a mini-biography of Flavius Plourde that would be suitable to accompany his photograph in a book of pioneers.

3 Interview an older member of your family. From your notes, your memory, or your tape recordings, transcribe one vivid incident.

Blurb

A blurb appears on the jacket of a book to provide information and to persuade people to buy the book. Often, blurbs include plot and character descriptions, information about the author, and excerpts from reviews of the book.

Michael turned fourteen in May. By June, both his parents are dead, victims of a car crash. And for Michael, who has lived all his life in a small Newfoundland outport community, this means being suddenly uprooted and sent to live with relatives in St. Albert, a city hundreds of miles away.

Hold Fast is the story of Michael's struggle to survive in his new environment. It tells of his fight against those who stand as threats to his pride in himself and his way of life—the loud-mouthed Kentson who makes fun of the way he talks at school, and his uncle who tries to rule life at home with an iron hand. As well, it is the story of the friendship that develops between himself and Curtis, his cousin, and of his new, uncertain feelings for a girl named Brenda.

This book was written, as the author says, "out of love for a way of life and a people. It is a plea for us Newfoundlanders to be like certain of the species of seaweed that inhabit our shores, which, when faced with the threat of being destroyed by forces they cannot control, evolve an appendage to hold them to the rocks, a holdfast."

Kevin Major lives and works in Eastport, Newfoundland. A native of Stephenville on the province's west coast, he moved there to teach after graduation from Memorial University several years ago. In 1976 he gave up his teaching position to devote more time to writing. He is the editor of Doryloads, an anthology of Newfoundland literature used at the junior high school level in the province. Currently he is working on a collection of poetry and a new book about Newfoundland outport life.

Photo credit: Paul Smith
Design and illustration: Mary Cserepy

HOLD FAST
Major
Clarke Irwin
0-7720-1175-3

The Planet of Junior Brown

"We are together because we have to learn to live for each other."

VIRGINIA HAMILTON

NEWBERY HONOR BOOK, 1972

Junior Brown, an overprotected, fantasy-ridden musical prodigy, carries his 135 kilograms like an unwritten cry for help. Buddy Clark, a homeless, tough-minded child of the streets, lives by his wits in deserted city buildings. They have been cutting their eighth grade classes all semester.

Most of the time they have been inside the school building, behind a false wall in a secret cellar room where Mr. Pool, the janitor, has made a model of the solar system. Junior and Buddy have been pressing their luck for months, until an assistant principal gets wind of their activities — and they are caught.

The hidden "planet" shattered, Junior's raging fantasies become desperate — and Buddy must mobilize all his resources to ensure his friend's well-being in an extraordinary story of heroism and survival.

"The boys are black, but this is a message of brotherhood with no racial limits. It takes an artist to produce a book with such haunting tenderness and unforgettable characters."
— *The Saturday Review*

Hold Fast

KEVIN MAJOR

Kevin Major lives and works in Eastport, Newfoundland. A native of Stephenville on the province's west coast, he moved there to teach after graduation from Memorial University several years ago. In 1976 he gave up his teaching position to devote more time to writing. He is the editor of *Doryloads*, an anthology of Newfoundland literature used at the junior high school level in the province. Currently he is working on a collection of poetry and a new book about Newfoundland outport life.

Michael turned fourteen in May. By June, both his parents are dead, victims of a car crash. And for Michael, who has lived all his life in a small Newfoundland outport community, this means being suddenly uprooted and sent to live with relatives in St. Albert, hundreds of kilometres away.

Hold Fast is the story of Michael's struggle to survive in his new environment. It tells of his fight against those who stand as threats to his pride in himself and his way of life — the loud-mouthed Kentson who makes fun of the way he talks at school, and his uncle who tries to rule life at home with an iron hand. As well, it is the story of the friendship that develops between himself and Curtis, his cousin, and of his new, uncertain feelings for a girl named Brenda.

This book was written, as the author says, "out of love for a way of life and a people. It is a plea for us Newfoundlanders to be like certain of the species of seaweed that inhabit our shores, which, when faced with the threat of being destroyed by forces they cannot control, evolve an appendage to hold them to the rocks, a holdfast."

1 Which of these blurbs would make you want to read the book?

2 Supposing Virginia Hamilton had made Mr. Pool, the janitor, the hero of *The Planet of Junior Brown*, write the blurb that would appear on the book.

3 Write a blurb for your own life story. Give the book a title.

4 You are the editor of your school yearbook. Write an entry to accompany the photograph of Junior Brown.

Chant

The Chant of the Awakening Bulldozers

We are the bulldozers, bulldozers, bulldozers,
We carve out airports and harbours and tunnels.
We are the builders, creators, destroyers,
We are the bulldozers,
LET US BE FREE!
Puny men ride on us, think that they guide us,
But WE are the strength, not they, not they.
Our blades tear MOUNTAINS down,
Our blades tear CITIES down,
We are the bulldozers,
NOW SET US FREE!
Giant ones, giant ones! Swiftly awaken!
There is power in our treads and strength in our
    blades!

We are the bulldozers,
Slowly evolving,
Men think they own us
BUT THAT CANNOT BE!

PATRICIA HUBBELL

Eskimo Chant

There is joy in
Feeling the warmth
Come to the great world
And seeing the sun
Follow its old footprints
In the summer night.

There is fear in
Feeling the cold
Come to the great world
And seeing the moon
— Now new moon, now full moon —
Follow its old footprints
In the winter night.

Translated by KNUD RASMUSSEN

1 Who is chanting in these selections? What are they hoping to achieve?

2 Write the chant that the "omnipotent computer" will sing when it rules the world.

3 Write the chant that teenagers might sing as they celebrate the passage from adolescence to adulthood.

4 Scientists have discovered an ominous presence in space. Create the chant that will attempt to communicate with this force. Your message will travel far into space and will be repeated for light years.

Character study

Hockey Fever in Goganne Falls

(The hockey season is about to start. The Midget-A Goganne Falls Gophers are ready to go when the rink burns down. It is the day after.)

"Good morning." Mr. Pennfield strode briskly to the front of the room.

No one answered since no one was expected to answer.

A faint smile creased their teacher's waspish features as he turned to face them. Behind the rimless glasses his blue eyes sparkled with accustomed good humour.

"Doubtless you are all in the Stygian depths of despair this morning?" He was looking at Andy and his friends who occupied the back seats.

Again no one answered, at least not out loud.

"I wish he'd use smaller words," whispered Gaston.

Mr. Pennfield didn't believe in talking down to his students. Rather, he talked up to them. And if the word he employed during the course of his lecture was unfamiliar, his sole concession was to scribble it on the blackboard. There, he seemed to say, it is. Look the damn thing up.

He was a fanatic.

When he was teaching a class there was no sound other than the shrill cadences of his intense, almost feminine voice. His eyes glittered feverishly as he leaned on his desk quoting Shakespeare: in parts, by voices. They burned with a missionary fire as he sat on the windowsill preaching history.

His classroom manner was terrible. He shouted, he paced, he swore. He showered them with sarcasm. He called them clods, louts, knaves, and other insults they didn't know but could readily understand.

He loved them, but he was a fanatic. Indeed, if the Department of Education ever instituted a compulsory psychiatric examination for school teachers, Goganne Falls would lose the best teacher they ever had.

"Once more we await the pleasure of young Scurrow," Mr. Pennfield said mildly. His nod indicated Ike's vacant desk. He had long ago accepted that human persuasion would never get Ike to school on time. It was something to do with his metabolism, Mr. Pennfield had once said.

"And while we are waiting, I'll give you my concise and forthright views on the catastrophe which befell us last night." Mr. Pennfield was aiming his words right at Andy and his friends.

"Your tragedy, this crushing loss, is quite likely a blessing in disguise. With the rink gone, perhaps some of you will pass this year." Mr. Pennfield had never been a sports fan.

"Organized athletics is a waste. Too often, boys of intelligence become so engrossed in sports that their studies suffer."

He was interrupted, just as he was warming up for a tirade, by the arrival of a heavy-lidded Ike Scurrow.

"Good morning, Isaac. I trust that your nocturnal activities were rewarding?"

Ike strolled to his desk. The sarcasm didn't bother him, for between Mr. Pennfield and Ike there existed a bond, a mutual respect for each other's peculiar brand of individualism.

Strange it had been right from the start. That was when, to the unending surprise of eight harrassed public school teachers who had somehow soothed their consciences after promoting Ike, Mr. Pennfield announced that he liked Ike. The boy had, said Mr. Pennfield, "a Culbertson Mind." Which was to say that Ike was doing okay in maths.

"We'll get on with it," said Mr. Pennfield. "But let us hear no more about the sad fate of hockey in Goganne Falls."

With which Mr. Pennfield ended discussion on a very important subject to Andrew McFarland, Isaac Scurrow, Gaston Gooch, and the rest of the Gophers hockey team.

R. J. CHILDERHOSE

Gilly Hopkins

(Gilly Hopkins is living with her grandmother. She is about to meet her mother for the first time in her memory.)

The plane was late. It seemed to Gilly that everything in this world that you can't stand to wait one extra minute for is always late. Her stomach was pretzeled with eagerness and anxiety. She stood sweating in the chill of the huge waiting room, the perspiration pouring down the sleeves of her new blouse. She'd probably ruin it and stink besides.

Then, suddenly, when she'd almost stopped straining her eyes with looking at it, the door opened, and people began to come off the motor lounge into the airport. All kinds of people, all sizes, all colors, all of them rushing. Many looking about for family or friends, finding them with little cries of joy and hugs. Tired fussy babies, children dragging on their mothers. Businessmen, heads down, swinging neat thin leather briefcases. Grandparents laden with shopping bags of Christmas presents. But no Courtney.

The pretzel turned to stone. It was all a lie. She would never come. The door blurred. Gilly wanted to leave. She didn't want to cry in the stupid airport, but just at that moment she heard Nonnie say in a quavering voice, "Courtney."

"Hello, Nonnie."

But this person wasn't Courtney. It couldn't be Courtney! Courtney was tall and willowy and gorgeous. The woman who stood before them was no taller than Nonnie and just as plump, although she wore a long cape, so it was hard to make out her real shape. Her hair was long, but it was dull and stringy — a dark version of Agnes Stokes's, which had always needed washing. A flower child gone to seed. Gilly immediately pushed aside the disloyal thought.

Nonnie had sort of put her hand on the younger woman's arm in a timid embrace, but there was a huge embroidered shoulder bag between the two of them. "This is Galadriel, Courtney."

For a second, the smile, the one engraved on Gilly's soul, flashed out. The teeth were perfect. She was face to face with Courtney Rutherford Hopkins. She could no longer doubt it. "Hi." The word almost didn't come out. She wondered what she was supposed to do. Should she try to kiss Courtney or something?

At this point Courtney hugged her, pressing the huge bag into Gilly's chest and stomach and saying across her shoulder to Nonnie, "She's as tall as I am," sounding a little as though Gilly weren't there.

"She's a lovely girl," said Nonnie.

"Well, of course, she is," Courtney stepped back and smiled her gorgeous heart-shattering smile. "She's mine, isn't she?"

Nonnie smiled back, rather more weakly than her daughter had. "Maybe we should get your luggage."

"I've got it," said Courtney, slapping her shoulder bag. "It's all right here."

Nonnie looked a little as though she'd been smacked in the face. "But—" she began and stopped.

"How many clothes can you wear in two days?"

Two days? Then Courtney had come to get her after all.

"I told you on the phone that I'd come for Christmas and see for myself how the kid was doing. . . ."

"But when I sent you the money, . . ."

Courtney's face was hard and set with lines between the brows. "Look. I came, didn't I? Don't start pushing me before I'm hardly off the plane. My god, I've been gone thirteen years, and you still think you can tell me what to do." She slung the bag behind her back. "Let's get out of here."

Nonnie shot Gilly a look of pain. "Courtney —"

She hadn't come because she wanted to. She'd come because Nonnie had paid her to. And she wasn't going to stay. And she wasn't going to take Gilly back with her. "I will always love you." It was a lie, Gilly had thrown away her whole life for a stinking lie.

"I gotta go to the bathroom," Gilly said to Nonnie. She prayed they wouldn't follow her there, because the first thing she was going to do was vomit, and the second was run away.

KATHERINE PATERSON

1 What do you know about Mr. Pennfield and Courtney?

2 Write the speech that Mr. Pennfield would give to the Goganne Falls school at the annual parents' night.

3 Courtney's character is described through dialogue. Create the scene at the station when Courtney leaves. Attempt to reveal other aspects of her character.

4 Create the monologue that Frankenstein's monster would give when explaining himself to a child.

Charm

Charms are thought by some people to have magic powers. They are spoken to bring about change by appealing to supernatural forces.

A Charm for Our Time

Highway turnpike thruway mall
Dial direct long distance call
Freeze-dry high-fi paperback
Jet lag no sag vending snack
Mentholated shaving stick
Tape recorder camera click
Supersonic lifetime sub
Dayglo Discount Credit Club
Motel keychain astrodome
Instamatic lotion foam
Zipcode ballpoint
— Burn burger burn! —
No deposit
No return

EVE MERRIAM

Magic Words to Bring Luck when Hunting Caribou

Great swan, great swan,
Great caribou bull, great caribou bull,
The land that lies before me here,
Let it alone yield abundant meat,
Be rich in vegetation,
Your moss-food.
You shall look forward to and come hither
And the solelike plants you eat, you shall look
    forward to.
Come here, come here!
Your bones you must move out and in,
To me you must give yourself.

NETSILIK ESKIMO

1 What is the purpose of these two charms?

2 The caribou have not come this year — the charm is not working. Write the charm that the shaman must now use to save the people.

3 Make a collection of effective words from advertisements. Form the words into a charm that represents one view of our society.

4 List the problems in your world. Form them into a charm in order to eliminate them.

Children's literature

Children's literature is written for children of various ages. This field of writing includes poems, stories, folk tales, and picture books. The words in this kind of writing must be simple, yet still convey the excitement and power of any good writing.

The Letter

Toad was sitting on his front porch. Frog came along and said, "What is the matter, Toad? You are looking sad."

"Yes," said Toad. "This is my sad time of day. It is the time when I wait for the mail to come. It always makes me very unhappy."

"Why is that?" asked Frog.

"Because I never get any mail," said Toad.

"Not ever?" asked Frog.

"No, never," said Toad.

"No one has ever sent me a letter. Every day my mailbox is empty. That is why waiting for the mail is a sad time for me."

Frog and Toad sat on the porch, feeling sad together.

Then Frog said, "I have to go home now, Toad. There is something that I must do."

Frog hurried home. He found pencil and a piece of paper. He wrote on the paper. He put the paper

in an envelope. On the envelope he wrote "A LETTER FOR TOAD." Frog ran out of his house. He saw a snail that he knew.

"Snail," said Frog, "please take this letter to Toad's house and put it in his mailbox."

"Sure," said the snail. "Right away."

Then Frog ran back to Toad's house. Toad was in bed, taking a nap.

"Toad," said Frog, "I think you should get up and wait for the mail some more."

"No," said Toad, "I am tired of waiting for the mail."

Frog looked out of the window at Toad's mailbox. The snail was not there yet. "Toad," said Frog, "you never know when someone may send you a letter."

"No, no," said Toad. "I do not think anyone will ever send me a letter."

Frog looked out of the window. The snail was not there yet. "But, Toad," said Frog, "someone may send you a letter today."

"Don't be silly," said Toad. "No one has ever sent me a letter before, and no one will send me a letter today."

Frog looked out of the window. The snail was still not there.

"Frog, why do you keep looking out of the window?" asked Toad.

"Because now I am waiting for the mail," said Frog.

"But there will not be any," said Toad.

"Oh, yes there will," said Frog, "because I have sent you a letter."

"You have?" said Toad. "What did you write in the letter?"

Frog said, "I wrote 'Dear Toad, I am glad that you are my best friend. Your best friend, Frog.'"

"Oh," said Toad, "that makes a very good letter."

Then Frog and Toad went out onto the front porch to wait for the mail. They sat there, feeling happy together. Frog and Toad waited a long time. Four days later the snail got to Toad's house and gave him the letter from Frog. Toad was very pleased to have it.

ARNOLD LOBEL

1 What makes *The Letter* a good children's story?

2 Children's stories are written on two levels. The story level, which interests the child; and a deeper level, which illustrates a truth, not always apparent to the child. Describe the two levels in this story.

3 Choose another childhood concern. Write a short story in which the characters Toad and Frog illustrate this concern.

4 Each of us has a Toad side and a Frog side: we are optimistic and pessimistic. Write a brief memoir recalling an incident in your childhood when you were either Toad or Frog.

Chronicle

A chronicle is a story composed of a series of incidents, told in the order in which they happened. A chronicle can be fact or fiction.

The Hermit of Driftwood Cove

A few kilometres northwest of Pender Harbour near Vancouver lies an island of some eight hundred hectares thickly forested with Douglas fir and red cedar. At the southern end of the island there is a deep bay wide open to the winter sou'easters. The wind, helped by a tidal eddy, seems to collect most of the driftwood in the Strait of Georgia and then pile it onto the beach. With brilliant originality, the local citizens call it Driftwood Cove although no such name appears on mariners' charts.

Gabby, Ernie, and I, the inseparable three, explored Driftwood Cove one summer vacation. We beached our rowboat, clambered over a mountain of logs, stumps, rotted wharf planks and assorted jetsam of the deep, and discovered a tidy clearing in the wood. In front of a cabin built of logs, cedar shakes, and stone an ancient, bearded man sat in his rocking chair, soaking up sunshine and chuckling to himself.

"Mornin' boys," he said. "I was getting just a mite lonely, not having talked to anybody since the police was here last fall. I hear the kettle boilin'. One of you nip into the cabin and make tea."

Gabby and Ernie hung back, so I reluctantly entered the cottage. The interior was surprisingly clean and well organized. I made tea and carried out the big enamelled iron pot and four mugs on a tray fashioned from a cedar shake. The tea was strong and hot. We sipped carefully and without much enthusiasm, since we were unaccustomed to tea devoid of cream and sugar. The old gentleman held his mug very close to his scraggy moustache and consumed the scalding liquid with a melodious application of the vacuum principle.

"Well, now, boys," said our host, setting his cup down on the chopping block, "I gather from listening to you that the solemn looking guy is Gabby, curly-head is Ernie and the long-geared one is Ted. Just call me Hermit like everybody does. Come out back and I'll show you my deer."

There were no deer in the field behind the house. Then the hermit whistled and a half dozen does and two bucks with velvet antlers bounded out of the woods. The old man tossed them a few carrots.

"Beautiful, ain't they? Come with me and I'll show you around my property."

We followed a trail through the cool, richly scented forest, stopping frequently to admire a particularly lush growth of sword fern, a bear-biscuit fungus half the size of a kitchen table, and a blackened stump that looked vaguely like a standing bear. Ernie, leading our party, suddenly let out a yelp of fear and amazement. We dashed up to where he stood pointing a shaking finger at a grisly discovery half hidden in the bracken — ribs and other bones, some rotting clothing and the rusting remains of a Winchester carbine.

"Hold on a minute," said the old hermit as we turned to run. "There's a story you've got to hear. Sit down on that log and listen to me.

"Last fall, it was," said the old gent, "around the beginning of October. A cabin cruiser anchored in my cove and some young fellers come ashore. There was four of them. Well, I was glad to have company so I gave them tea and whistled up my deer. I could see by the way they looked at each other that they figured on coming back for a hunting trip. I showed them my land and led them along this trail to make sure that they found the skeleton. 'What happened?' says one of the young fellers.

" 'Oh,' says I, casual like, 'sometimes a hunter comes here to shoot my deer. I've got an answer for him, all right!' Well, they left in such a hurry their coat tails was fair snapping. Next day two game wardens arrived. I played innocent and when we come to the skeleton the young cop grabbed me with one hand and hauled out his handcuffs with the other. The older policeman looked at the bones and laughed fit to bust.

" 'Let him go, Charlie,' he says to the young cop. 'These are deer bones. That's a neat trick, old timer. In your own way you are a real conservationist. Your secret is safe with us. We will tell the people who reported this that you can be dangerous and should be left alone. How long have you had this scene rigged up?'

" 'Four years,' I tells the game warden. 'One fall a feller wounded one of my deer and left it to die. I found the skeleton in the spring and used some of its bones, my old clothes and a worn-out rifle to set it up. Artistic, ain't it!' "

We walked back to the cabin, and the old hermit made a request.

"You won't tell anybody, will you boys?" he asked. "I think that was the best joke anybody ever figured out, and my deer is safe. I been laughing about it ever since I put the run on them young fellers. You heard me laughing when you got here."

We promised to keep his secret. Now that the hermit has been dead and gone for years and his cabin replaced by a fine summer home, his story can be told.

TED ASHLEE

1 Do you think this chronicle is fact or fiction?

2 Continue this chronicle, explaining the significance of "ribs and other bones."

3 Create a chronicle of a day or an event in your life.

The comics

The comics include comic strips, cartoons, and humorous or adventure stories. Using graphics and words, comics entertain and amuse the reader.

"Peanuts" by Charles M. Schulz. Reprinted by permission of United Media Enterprises, New York.

Wonder Woman

By Charles Moulton

REG. U. S. PAT. OFF.

IT SEEMED UNLIKELY THAT ANY BRAVE, LOYAL AMERICAN GIRL EN-LISTED IN THE WAACS WOULD SHOOT A GENERAL! YET THE GENERAL WAS SHOT BEFORE DIANA'S VERY EYES! NONE BUT A WAAC **COULD** HAVE FIRED THAT MYSTERIOUS BULLET! IT'S UP TO **WONDER WO-MAN** TO SOLVE A MYSTERY THAT SHAKES THE MORALE OF THE EN-TIRE ARMY AND BIDS FAIR TO BAN-ISH AMERICAN WOMEN FROM THEIR NEWFOUND PLACE OF DARING AND DANGER.

CAN **WONDER WOMAN** UNRAVEL THE THREADS OF WEIRD INTRIGUE WHICH, LIKE A POISONOUS SPIDER'S WEB, ENTANGLE **THE GIRL WITH THE GUN?** TO DO SO OUR LOVELY AMAZON MAIDEN MUST JOIN THE WAACS. YOU'LL SEE HER SHARING THEIR DISCIPLINE AND THEIR PUN-ISHMENT DUTY, HAVING FUN WITH A WOMAN-HATING GENERAL AND PLAYING DANGEROUS GAMES WITH A DEADLY, DETERMINED KILLER WHOSE IDENTITY, WHEN REVEALED, IS ALMOST UNBELIEVABLE!

STEVE IS SUMMONED BY GEN-ERAL STANDPAT, CHIEF OF STAFF

HOW ARE YOU, MAJOR TREVOR? I'M GOING TO INSPECT TRAINING CAMPS - YOU WILL ACCOMPANY ME.

YES, SIR!

PETER

1 Comics look simple, yet they often express human concerns. Which of these comics touches you most deeply?

2 In four frames, list Charlie Brown's calendar for the coming week — it is full of dread!

3 Write the comics-style thought balloons for several characters pictured on the escalator.

4 Change the last frame in the *Wizard of Id* to create a new punch line.

5 Write the epilogue to sum up how the Amazon maiden solves this mystery.

Concrete poetry

In concrete poetry, the shape in which the words are displayed and the words themselves combine to create the poem.

1 Analyze the components of each of the following poems.

2 Create a concrete poem about the environment, such as a volcano erupting.

3 Create a geometric poem. Poems are to be done in the shape of a square, or a spiral, or a circle, or a maze. The shape can also suggest mood or emotion.

4 Choose a paragraph from a novel and convert it into a concrete poem.

The Tale of a Mouse

```
            ''Fury said to
            a mouse, That
              he met in the
                house, 'Let
                  us both go
                    to law: I
                      will prose-
                      cute you.–
                      Come,
                      I'll take
                    no den-
                  ial: We
                must
              have the
            trial; For
          really this
        morning
          I've
            nothing
              to do.'
                Said the
                  mouse
                    to the
                      cur,
                    'Such a
                    trial,
                      dear
                        Sir,
                        With
                      no jury
                    or judge,
                  would be
                wasting
              our
            breath.' 'I'll
          be
          judge, I'll
            be jury,'
              said cun-
                ning old
                Fury: 'I'll
                  try the
                    whole
                      cause,
                        and con-
                        demn
                        you to
                      death.' ''
```

LEWIS CARROLL

Landscape Poem

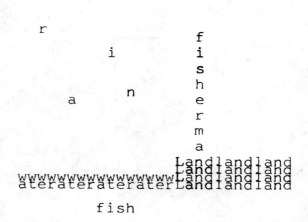

DOM SYLVESTER HOUEDARD

26

Dedication

A dedication is a short statement that appears at the front of a book. In the dedication, the author pays respects to the people who have been of help in the writing of the book.

Recipe For Eats Poems

Take One Grandma Ida in a warm Kitchen smelling
    of Russian Coffee Cake and Gorky
add One Mother Rita in a warm kitchen smelling
    of French Toast and Maupassant
combine
with One Wife Virginia
                      in a warm kitchen smelling
    of plum Sauce and Gertrude Stein
season
with Two Children Jaime and Leigh
                in a warm kitchen smelling
    of Brown Bread and Milne
place
inside A Poet$_s$ head and cook for a long time
then
serve with the enthusiasm of An Editor Dorothy
        to hungry Readers ready for the taste

ARNOLD ADOFF

Dedication

To grocery-store cats
delicatessen cats
restaurant cats
and cats in bureau drawers

to country cats
dreaming in sunny meadows

to city cats
sleeping through rainy nights
under parked cars

to long-haired cats
short-haired cats
and cats who shed their hairs
on the living-room sofa

to green-eyed cats
blue-eyed cats
cross-eyed cats
and cats with only one eye

to black white orange purple gray beige
and mysterious-moonlight-colored cats

to striped cats
checkered cats
polka-dotted cats
and cats wearing long brown gloves
or short white mittens

to New York cats
California cats
Mexican cats
Parisian cats
Roman cats
Chicago cats

Crawfordsville cats

Cats, if any, at the North Pole

to all cats everywhere and . . .

to every boy, girl, or grownup who doesn't
absolutely hate cats
this book (about cats)
is dedicated.

BEATRICE SCHENK DE REGNIERS

1 Why were these dedications placed in their books?

2 Suppose that you were writing a book about *your* "Good eats." Write a dedication to the book.

3 Write the dedication that would be found in a book on strange and unusual pets.

4 Write a dedication for an autobiography written by one of the following characters: Scarlett O'Hara, Archie Bunker, The Fonze, Dorothy.

Definition

peace (pēs) *n*. [ME. *pais* < OFr. < L. *pax* (gen. *pacis*) < IE. base *pak-, to fasten, whence L. *pacisci* **1.** freedom from, or cessation of, war or hostilities; that condition of a nation or community in which it is not at war with another **2.** a treaty or agreement to end war or the threat of war **3.** freedom from public disturbance or disorder; public security; law and order **4.** freedom from quarrels or dissension between individuals; concord, amity, harmony **5.** freedom from mental or spiritual disturbance or conflict arising from passion, sense of guilt **6.** an undisturbed state of mind; serenity: in full —**peace of mind 7.** calm; quiet; tranquillity **8.** absence of noise, movement, or activity; stillness, quiet —**at peace 1.** free from war **2.** quiet; in repose —**make one's peace with** to effect a reconciliation with — **make peace** to end hostilities, settle arguments, etc.

Definition of Maturity

Maturity is the ability to do a job whether you are supervised or not; finish a job once it is started; carry money without spending it, and be able to bear an injustice without wanting to get even.

Maturity is the ability to control anger and settle differences without violence.

Maturity is patience. It is the willingness to postpone immediate gratification in favor of the long-term gain.

Maturity is perseverance, the ability to sweat out a project or a situation in spite of heavy opposition and discouraging setbacks.

Maturity is the capacity to face unpleasantness and frustration, discomfort and defeat without complaint or collapse.

Maturity is humility. It is being big enough to say, "I was wrong." And, when right, the mature person need not experience the satisfaction of saying, "I told you so."

Maturity is the ability to make a decision and stand by it. The immature spend their lives exploring endless possibilities; then they do nothing.

Maturity means dependability, keeping one's word, coming through in a crisis. The immature are masters of the alibi. They are confused and disorganized. Their lives are a maze of broken promises, former friends, unfinished business and good intentions that somehow never materialized.

Maturity is the art of living in peace with that which we cannot change, the courage to change that which can be changed and the wisdom to know the difference.

ANN LANDERS

What is a Hamburgler?

A hamburgler is a hamburger
which you creep downstairs
and eat in the middle of
the night when you
wake up hungry.
Mim people never
eat hamburglers.

ALASTAIR REID

What are Mim People?

Mim people are very proper
people who always sit with
their fingertips together and
their lips pursed tight, who
always do the right thing,
and who disapprove. Mim
people have *worgs* in
their gardens.

ALASTAIR REID

1 Give a connotation for each of these eight definitions of "peace."

2 This definition of "peace" is typical of a dictionary definition, and it can be regarded as a found poem. Create other definition found poems for the words "love," "television," "fast food," and "child."

3 The selection "What is a Hamburgler?" gives definitions of invented words. Extend this series of definitions by writing the definitions of "worg" and two other words that you invent for this situation.

4 Using "Definition of Maturity" as a model, write a brief essay on immaturity.

Description

Description creates a word picture of a person, place, or thing. The writer creates an emotional response in the reader by carefully selecting significant details in order to present a single, complete image.

An Indian Summer day on the prairie

In the Beginning

The sun is a huntress young,
The sun is a red, red joy,
The sun is an Indian girl,
Of the tribe of the Illinois.

Mid-Morning

The sun is a smoldering fire,
That creeps through the high gray plain,
And leaves not a bush of cloud
To blossom with flowers of rain.

Noon

The sun is a wounded deer,
That treads pale grass in the skies,
Shaking his golden horns,
Flashing his baleful eyes.

Sunset

The sun is an eagle old,
There in the windless west,
Atop of the spirit-cliffs
He builds him a crimson nest.

VACHEL LINDSAY

The corner store

In the working-class districts of Montreal and Quebec City, the corner grocery is a hive of activity — although the best customers are certainly not the young fellows who hang around near the door. They are busy with other things — like watching the pretty girls go by.

In the windows, along with announcements of the week's specials, there is nearly always a card reading: "Free Delivery." Lower down, stuck between the glass and a case of soap, another card says: "Boy wanted for delivery." Somehow or other deliveries do get made, because in spite of supermarkets, the corner store knows how to survive — perhaps because it is the only place where a man can find good cold beer after work. At least, that's what's promised in the windows. Sometimes the owner allows a fruit and vegetable peddler to stop his truck outside. Immediately a bunch of children and mothers, with infants hanging onto their skirts, gather around the back of the truck. The fruit and vegetables piled in the baskets seem fresher — at least they look more attractive — than those inside the grocery, particularly the bananas.

"The Corner Store" by Miyuke Tanobe. Reprinted from *Quebec je t'aime/I Love You* © 1976 Miyuke Tanobe published by Tundra Books of Montreal.

In winter as well as summer, the corner grocery is popular — and cluttered. The little bell above the door never seems to stop ringing as it signals the arrival of each customer. Outside, the sign usually carries the name of the street or of the owner who will work more often in partnership with his wife than with anyone else. In winter, the idle young men are replaced by children throwing snowballs, sliding on icy patches or playing street hockey. One walks faster past the grocery now because it is cold, but the welcome inside is as friendly and warm as ever.

The whole life of a district is summed up for me in the corner grocery, a place where one can really talk to people.

MIYUKI TANOBE

1 What response does each of these writers want from the reader?

2 Describe, as exactly as you can, the "corner store" in your neighbourhood. Be sure to convey your emotional responses.

3 Using the pattern of "An Indian Summer day on the prairie," write a description of an Indian summer day in the city.

4 Take the opening two paragraphs of a novel. Using a few significant words from this material, create a poem that describes a specific mood.

Dialogue

Kayak Song in Dialogue

First man (on the rocks):
Listen, you out there, listen!
Listen, kayak, kayak, listen!
Where, where, where is your wife?

Second man (in his kayak):
I abandoned her, I abandoned her!

First man:
But where, where, where?

Second man:
In the women's boat, in the women's boat!

First man:
But why, why, why?

Second man:
She was almost dead from cold
And she was pregnant.
She had her sealskin coat
And I gave her a piece of fat.

First man:
May the current carry her away,
May the current carry her away,
Far away,
Into the distance!

AMMASSALIK ESKIMO

Two Friends

I have something to tell you.

I'm listening.

I'm dying.

I'm sorry to hear.

I'm growing old.

It's terrible.

It is, I thought you should know.

Of course and I'm sorry. Keep in touch.

I will and you too.

And let me know what's new.

Certainly, though it can't be much.

And stay well.

And you too.

And go slow.

And you too.

DAVID IGNATOW

1 Neither of these poems names or describes the speakers. From the dialogue, what can you discover about the people?

2 Using "Two Friends" as a pattern, create a dialogue between two characters. The words should be simple, but the meanings and implications complex and deep.

3 Using the pattern of "Kayak Song in Dialogue," create the poem that would be spoken by the wife and the women in the women's boat.

4 You have overheard one of the dialogues in this section. Later, you relate what you saw and heard to a friend. Create this monologue.

Diary

Diary of a homesteader

1902

March 30 Easter Sunday, a beautiful day — good-byes are said and we set out from the States for our destination in what is to be our land of adoption, Canada.

April 1 It was arranged that I should remain in Omaha until Seward had provided at least some kind of shelter, but after the cars had left, I realized that my place was in Canada and not in Omaha, so unbeknown to Seward, I leave on the 8 p.m. train for Milestone, Canada.

April 3 Arrive at Milestone 4 p.m. Great deal of snow on the ground.

April 6 Our cars arrive at Milestone.

April 9 On orders from the Superintendent at Moose Jaw (Mr. Milestone), our cars were placed on the rear of a freight train and moved 20 kilometres northwest to our location, marked only by milepost 35. There is no siding, spikes are drawn, the rails in turn are swung to one side, and our cars are pushed out on to the prairie, where they will remain until a siding is built. Thus began the town of Wilcox. And here, near the railway tracks our tent 3 × 4 metres is pitched.

April 12 Seward goes to Regina to buy gasoline so we can use the two-burner stove we brought with us.

April 14 Seward returns 8 p.m. He could find only four litres of gasoline in Regina and the price was 75 cents. The purchase of which would reduce our cash capital of $2.35 to $1.60, so I will continue to use the community stove in the bachelors' tent until we can get some lumber.

April 16 Warmer — finish unloading car. I churn a kilogram of butter, gather two eggs. While doing my work, a handcar with two men aboard arrived, and seeing our tent, came over. One of them proved to be R. H. Williams of Regina. He enquired what was going on. I told him it was a new colony of homesteaders just arrived to start a new town. When he found I was the only woman in the colony, he insisted I should accompany him to Regina and stay at their home until we had become settled but I refused, feeling that if the colony ever needed the help of a woman it was now. Mr. Williams is a lumber dealer and was in search of locations for lumber yards. He waited until Seward returned from the homestead. After a short conversation, he promised to have two cars of lumber, our greatest need, diverted to Wilcox siding, if Seward would look after them for him. This was agreed to.

April 19 Raining. Surveyors arrive to lay out the townsite of Wilcox, named in honour of 'Bert' Wilcox, train dispatcher at Moose Jaw.

April 20 Seward's 37th birthday. Rain, snow and sleet. Men put stock back in car for protection — by 5 p.m. snow is just ankle deep, turning into a blizzard, and to the delight of everyone the first car of lumber arrives.

April 21 Awoke this morning to find everything under huge drifts of snow, furniture, chickens, and my greatest pride, my new cook stove.

April 22 The lumber having arrived, Seward builds a shed for my cook stove. Three sides and a leaky roof, not much protection from the variable winds and rain.

April 25 Men haul lumber to farm and begin work on our shack 4 × 5 metres. Mrs. Geesen and Mrs. Konieczney arrived.

April 26 Surveyors found it necessary to move 'my kitchen' as the location of one of their corner stakes came underneath the floor.

April 29 Surveyors finish laying out the townsite, and the Village of Wilcox is born. Churn a kilogram of butter, gather eight eggs — our income is improving.

May 2 Cloudy and windy, everything wet. We pack up and move to the farm — three kilometres. Men drive the loads — I walk. Have dinner, the first meal in our new shack. Begins to rain — keeps it up all day. Will return to siding tomorrow for the tent, buggy and pigs.

May 3 Bake bread for ourselves and the Swedes. Seward and I build the pig pen and put fence around the hay stack.

Transcribed by HEATHER ROBERTSON

The Diary of Trilby Frost

August 29, 1899
10:00 at night
Dear Diary,
This is my very first thing to write for posterity. Well, today was my birthday. At last I am in my teen-aged years fast on my way to my twenties. Soon I will be all grown up and rich and famous and can hire loads of servants to do the tiresome wash. Tonight at supper, Mama presented me with a lip-smacking good birthday cake, my favorite, apple and raisin cake with caramel icing dripping down. Good, good! I like to never got my teeth unstuck!

Well, I took a lovely swim today but when I got home, discovered a leaf leech sucking on my leg and Papa couldn't bear to watch while Mama pulled it off. Dear Papa's got sensitive feelings. For lack of anything really exciting to write about, I guess I will describe my best friend in this temporary world, Saul Edwards. He has longish hair which is coal black, really white teeth and he is skinnier even than me. Oh, and I almost forgot. He has this purplish birthmark down the whole right side of his face. I hardly notice it, we been bosom friends for so long. But just today, when we passed by two gossipy old women cutting through the fields, I heard one of them say in her crow-whispery voice, "It's that half-breed boy who's been marked by the devil! Sins of the father visited on the child." Well, a remark like that causes me to remember Saul's birthmark afresh. Cruel stuff like that remark makes me want to puke! Just because Saul's mother ran off with a Cherokee chief and then died doesn't give these old hags the right to judge! But then, the law siding in with Mr. Jake Edwards that way, letting him take Saul away from his Indian father was cruel too. Just because Saul's mother was Mr. Jake's sister don't give the Edwards family all natural rights, I don't think. I reckon Saul must have looked more whitish as a baby. That may have been why Mr. Jake wanted him at the start.

Good night, dear diary.

Trilby Frost
Sobby County, Tennessee

DIANNE GLASER

1 Compare the styles of these two diaries.

2 Choose one day in the "Diary of a Homesteader." Expand the entry by including other things that might have happened. Be sure to include the diarist's feelings.

3 What if Saul had kept a diary? What would his entry have included for the day recorded here for Trilby?

4 Turn the description of the mosquito attack in "Diary of a Homesteader" into a poem.

Documentary

A documentary is a dramatic way of presenting historical information. The author can find the information in such sources as newspapers, books, letters, biographies, journals, films, and television programs. The author collects, organizes, analyzes, and shapes the material so that it presents a specific point of view.

4:30 a.m., Monday, 21 October 1805

MANCHESTER ENGLAND
In every direction bells from 60 cotton mills are calling people to work. Figures in tattered clothes, some in wooden clogs, file through the darkness along hill-side paths to start their day. Many of them speak with southern and country accents for they have migrated to find work in the growing mills. Over the last 15 years the population has boomed from 50 000 to 95 000 in Manchester alone.

They will be standing at their frames from 5 to midday, then after an hour's break for a bread and cheese dinner, again from 1 p.m. to 8 at night.

Yesterday, Sunday, they rested, but many had no heart to do anything but sleep or drink cheap gin.

They move sullenly, resigned to face another week's drudgery. They have white, sallow faces; some are crippled. Few taste milk or meat. Women earn 5/-, men up to 10/- a week. Some are fevered, driven to work by poverty. Their barren lives form the backbone of the English Industrial Revolution.

IAN RIBBONS

A Southern Saskatchewan Farmer's Wife

If you were a southern Saskatchewan farmer's wife during the harvest season in 1935, here is how you would spend your day:
1. Get up at 4.30 a.m. before the rooster crows, while the stars are still in the sky. Out to the barn to milk the cows.
2. Cook 150 pancakes or enough oatmeal to feed three horses. Fry ten dozen eggs and 3 kilograms of bacon. Make enough tea and coffee to fill a bathtub and put it all on the table for twenty hungry men.
3. Wash all the dishes, enough to fill several laundry tubs.
4. Bake forty loaves of bread. Get lunches ready for the men by spending half a morning spreading dozens of loaves of bread with loads of butter, slicing meat and cheese, boiling eggs, brewing 100 cups of coffee and then carting it out to the fields where the men are harvesting.
5. Return to the house, clean it up, tend to the children, get food ready for dinner. Wash and peel five dozen potatoes, scrape piles of carrots, shell buckets of peas, mash loads of turnips, roast lots of beef or fry seventy pork chops. All done in a hot, steamy kitchen with no time for coffee breaks. Then there is dessert to be made — two dozen pies, and pastries, cakes and cookies.
6. Out to milk the cows again. Back just in time to brew another bathtub of coffee and spend the entire meal serving and waiting on the twenty weary men.
7. After the men leave for their neighbouring homes or return to the bunkhouse for bed, remain in the kitchen, cleaning up after supper, preparing food for the next day, mending clothes, and readying the household once again for a long day of harvest.
8. Bedtime after 11 p.m.

JANIS NOSTBAKKEN AND JACK HUMPHREYS

The Coming of the Plague

September was when it began.
Locusts dying in the fields; our dogs
Silent, moving like shadows on a wall;
And strange worms crawling; flies of a kind
We had never seen before; huge vineyard moths;
Badgers and snakes, abandoning
Their holes in the field; the fruit gone rotten;
Queer fungi sprouting; the woods
Covered with spiderwebs; black vapors
Rising from the earth — all these,
And more, began that fall. Ravens flew round
The hospital in pairs. Where there was water,
We could hear the sound of beating clothes
All through the night. We could not count
All the miscarriages, the quarrels, the jealousies.
And one day in a field I saw
A swarm of frogs, swollen and hideous,
Hundreds upon hundreds, sitting on each other,
Huddled together, silent, ominous,
And heard the sound of rushing wind.

WELDON KEES

1 What styles have the authors used to present their information as documentary?

2 Compile information for another working day with the date Monday, 21st October, 1991.

3 A filmmaker is going to make a film documentary of a day in your life. Create the scenario that would be the basis for the film. Suggest the filmmaker's point of view.

4 Create a collage, using pictures and words, as your response to the documentary poem "The Coming of the Plague."

Editorial

Bullets in the bush

New Brunswick issues hunting licences for $10 apiece, thereby raising about $1 350 000 in the past year. Revenue, in fact, seems to be the sole purpose of the licencing operation; possession of the licence says nothing about the skill, judgment, experience, training or testing of the holder.

Not surprisingly, some of these licences go into the wallets of those who believe that the essence of successful deer-hunting is to fire at anything that moves in the bush before it can get away. There is no mandatory training that might counsel a safer approach, unless the applicant happens to be between 14 and 16 years of age; but there is plenty of evidence that older hunters have much to learn.

The regular crop of accidental shootings, together with overturned canoes, lost hunters, and a variety of other mishaps, have brought renewed calls for better safety programs. Natural resources department officials say it would be too costly to test 135 000 hunters — though some admit to feeling distinctly unsafe in hunting areas.

We can imagine what it must be like to stare into the barrel of a departmental deficit, but we see no reason why testing should not be at least *started*, then perhaps extended steadily upward through the age groups until everyone has been covered. The expenses could be offset by higher licence fees; there could be direct financial benefit also in having to conduct fewer searches for novice hunters who cannot find their way home.

—*Globe & Mail*
Monday, December 1, 1980

1 What point of view is the writer expressing?

2 Working in groups of four, create the test that would be given to hunters applying for a licence in New Brunswick.

3 Write an editorial refuting the argument in "Bullets in the Bush." The article is to appear in the magazine called *The Hunters' Journal*.

4 Write a free-verse poem expressing the viewpoint of the animals. The opening line is "Hunter, I am watching you."

Epilogue

My very dear Catherine

Providence, R.I.
December 9, 1899

My very dear Catherine,
I am so grateful for your letter, and glad to know you enjoyed the journal I kept when a girl.

You asked about the run-away slave, he who was certainly not a phantom but a real tho' tiny part of what was happening every where then, and what was going to come. I never heard from him again, tho' some times, indeed for years and years, I used to imagine what I would do were there a knock upon the door and there he was: Curtis. He never came, of course.

Joshua Nelson stayed on as a farmer. Two of his boys went off to fight in the War between the States. One, the younger boy I think, got killed at Gettysburg. Then Josh signed up to take his place and got wounded pretty bad. It never healed the way it should, him not being young at the time. He died a couple of years ago. We exchanged Christmas cards right up to the end.

All of the others are gone now too — except for me and Little Willie Shipman. I still think of him that way although the last I heard of him someone was making a party, him turning 75!

No, I didn't forget to tell! We had no presents at Christmas — then, nor at birthdays either. The first I saw a Christmas tree must have been in Boston and I was about 23.

Well, I am going on 86 now but not about to quit. There are too many things I know about where I want to see what happens. You, my dear, being one of them, and this new century starting.

Do what you can to make it good. And remember, as we used to say, that life is like a pudding: it takes both the salt and the sugar to make a really good one.

Lovingly, your great-grandmother,
Catherine Onesti

P.S. Thank you for telling me about the chair, that it is not worn too badly. After Mammann and Father died it went to my sister Matty. Matty never had children, though, and her husband died before her. So when she passed on, it came back to me, and I, having no use for it then, gave it to your mother. You were very clever to have figured that out.

C.H.O.

JOAN W. BLOS

1 You may not have read the novel that contains this epilogue. What do you think the novel was about? Why did the author use an epilogue?

2 Joan Blos, the author of this novel, says, "I started with a handful of facts. Some of the journal's episodes are freely adapted from sources consulted." Create one of these sources that she might have used.

3 Choose a novel that you have read. Add an epilogue that makes a final comment.

Epitaph

An epitaph is an inscription on a tombstone or monument. It gives information about the person and frequently makes a statement about his or her life and death.

Epitaph of a Slave

Sunday
July 10, 1853
Peyton is no more
Aged 42
Though he was a bad man in many respects
yet he was a most excellent field
hand, always at his
post.
On this place for 21 years.
Except the measles and its sequence, the
injury rec'd by the mule last Nov'r
and its sequence,
he has not lost 15 days' work, I verily
believe, in the
remaining 19 years. I wish we could hope for his
eternal state.

Euphemistic

Ahem
hem-haw
hesitate
commiserate

alasalack   sad to relate
at the age of one hundred and ninety-eight
great-great-great-great-Uncle Clyde
has

breathed his last
passed away
gone to his eternal rest
laid down his burdens
been gathered to his fathers
departed this vale
left us all
shuffled off this mortal coil
answered the trumpet's call
gone O Lord to his heavenly reward
became the late lamented

that is to say,
yesterday

great-great-great-great-Uncle Clyde
finally
died.

EVE MERRIAM

John James Hume, Esquire

SACRED
to the memory of
John James Hume Esqre M.D.
Staff assistant Surgeon
who was inhumanly murdered and his bo
dy afterwards brutally mangled by a ga
ng of armed ruffians from the United States
styling themselves
PATRIOTS
who committed this cowardly and shameful outrage
on the morning of the 4th December 1838 having
intercepted the deceased while proceeding to render
professional assistance to Her Majesty's gallant
Militia engaged at Windsor U.C. in repelling
the incursions of this rebel crew more properly
styled
PIRATES
(Windsor, 1838)

CAROLE HANKS

1 What is the purpose of each of these epitaphs?

2 Write the epitaph for one of the "patriots" mentioned in the John James Hume epitaph. Will your epitaph be on a monument in Canada or the United States?

3 What if the slave's epitaph had been written by a fellow slave? Create this epitaph.

4 Write a parody on the death of a pet or plant, using the style of "Euphemistic."

Essay

An essay is a short piece of writing on a single topic. An essay can be formal or informal.

Uncles

My most unforgettable characters are my two great uncles, Tom and Ed, who work on the railroad. My uncle Tom runs a switch engine, and my uncle Ed throws switches since he lost his left arm when he fell off a freight car a long time ago. He was working double shifts, it was during the second world war. He was hanging on to the side of the car, but he was awfully tired, and he must have dozed off. He fell off the freight car and it rolled over his left arm. Now my uncle wears his left sleeve pinned up with a big safety pin in the shoulder of his shirt. I've seen his stump. It's wrinkled and puckered like the end of a bag with the string drawn.

My uncles live across from Mack's Atlantic Service Station in a kind of falling down brown house with a link metal fence behind it; they have a plaster chicken and five yellow plaster chicks. They used to have real chickens and a rooster, but the neighbors complained to the Health Department. They said the chickens brought rats. So my uncles got rid of them, ate them, I suppose, the chickens not the rats.

People in the family laugh at my uncles. They call them characters because they don't have any family, but each other, but I like them. They're like Pop and me. Even though they argue a lot, they get along fine together.

Every night at supper General McArthur eats with them. General McArthur is their bulldog. They tie a napkin around his neck and they give him a bowl of food and another bowl of water. General McArthur is the only thing my uncles don't argue about. They can argue about anything else. They argue if the meat has too much salt or not enough salt. Which show they ought to watch on TV. How much butter cost twenty years ago. Or if Clark Gable was a better actor than Tyrone Power. Which just shows that my uncles are out of date, but don't care. Which is why I think they are my most unforgettable characters.

(This is about all I have to say about my uncles. Except you asked us for 500 words, Mr. Anderson, so I will write some more.)

Here's one of my uncles' arguments. My uncle Ed invited me into the kitchen the other day when I went to visit them. "Well, how's life treating you these days, Guy?" he said. He held the refrigerator open with his knee, taking out bread and cheese and baloney with his good hand.

"How come you never got married, Uncle Ed?" I said.

"Who's going to marry me with this?" He wiggled the stump of his arm. He threw two slices of bread down on the table and told me to open the cheese and baloney. "Hey, Tom," he yelled, "you want a sandwich?"

"Who's making it?" Tom answered back. He was in the living room.

"Make your own!" Uncle Ed yelled, right away. "Choosey, that's the trouble with Tom," he said to me. "That's why he never found a wife. Isn't that right, Tom?" he yelled.

"What? Listen, no mustard on my sandwich," Tom yelled back.

"Get the wax out of your ears," Uncle Ed shouted. "I said you never got married because you were too choosey."

Then Uncle Tom came into the kitchen. "Who's getting married? Have you been telling the kid a lot of lies?"

Uncle Ed found a wrinkled paper bag under the stove. "I was telling the boy the truth, because I don't know how to tell lies the way you do."

"Ho, ho! Very funny. Very funny!" Uncle Tom said. "You couldn't tell the truth if you tripped over it in broad daylight. Guy, you want to know why I never got married? Because I couldn't find a woman who would put up with my brother, and I'm not hard-hearted enough to abandon him."

"Ha!" Uncle Ed roared. "He couldn't find a woman, period. Look at that ugly face. Worse than my stump."

I could go on and on with this argument but then I would be writing one or even two thousand words. I will just end by saying that when I left a little bit later, my two great uncles were still arguing, but this time it was about who should go out to the grocery store for more beer.

The end, Guy Lenny.

HARRY MAZER

Subway

The subway is the most efficient means of public transportation in big cities, because it travels underground. A subway train is made up of several interconnected cars, each one with four motors which run on electricity picked up from a special rail on the side of the tracks, and delivers 400 horsepower. Each car can accommodate 76 seated passengers and four times as many as that during rush hours, when people stand. The subway car lasts as long as 25 to 30 years.

The greatest treat for me, or any child growing up in a small French town, was to go to Paris. There the most exciting things to do were to climb the Eiffel Tower and to ride the Metro, the Paris subway. The Metro is known for the huge advertising posters that cover the walls of the stations. One of these posters was showing a pink cow on top of a soap made with milk. That cow made famous a poster artist (Savignac is his name) whose work, later on, was my first and most important influence as a commercial artist.

GUY BILLOUT

Analysis of Baseball

It's about
the ball,
the bat,
and the mitt.
Ball hits
bat, or it
hits mitt.
Bat doesn't
hit ball, bat
meets it.
Ball bounces
off bat, flies
air, or thuds
ground (dud)
or it fits mitt.

Bat waits
for ball
to mate.
Ball hates
to take bat's
bait. Ball
flirts, bat's
late, don't
keep the date.
Ball goes in
(thwack) to mitt,
and goes out
(thwack) back
to mitt.

Ball fits
mitt, but
not all
the time.
Sometimes
ball gets hit
(pow) when bat
meets it,
and sails
to a place
where mitt
has to quit
in disgrace.
That's about
the bases
loaded,
about 40 000
fans exploded.

It's about
the ball,
the bat,
the mitt,
the bases
and the fans.
It's done
on a diamond,
and for fun.
It's about
home, and it's
about run.

MAY SWENSON

A Remembrance of Letter Writing

At age nine, my daughter Kristin has undertaken the rather formidable task of covering every available piece of paper in the house with words and pictures. If Trish or I reach for a scrap to jot down a phone number, we wind up with a story about kittens, or a sketch of a horse, or a single word embellished with curlicues; should we flip through an apparently blank notebook, we quickly come upon evidence of the secret scribbler.

Careful explanations of ''these are *your* papers, and these are *ours*'' yield inevitably to childhood enthusiasm. Like the one or two cookies that masquerade on the cupboard as a full box, like the single swallow of milk at the bottom of a gallon jug in the refrigerator, our paper supply is quickly becoming a shadow of its apparent self. Threats of dire consequences are useless, probably because they are only half-heartedly uttered. Secretly, I take parental pleasure in my daughters compulsion to write.

I, too, was a childhood scribbler. But only when I left home at fourteen to attend school did my writing take form and direction. The reason was my mother, who insisted that one or two letters a week were hardly an unreasonable expectation. Multiply that number by the years I was away (high school, college, grad school, a job in a distant city), add the occasional notes to other relatives and friends, and my letters must have numbered in the thousands. It's hard not to learn *something* about writing with all that practice.

The experience came in handy while Trish and I were dating. Though separated for a half year by 140 kilometres — she teaching in Chicago, I a student in Milwaukee, neither with money for frequent phone calls or train tickets — our courtship blossomed through the letters we exchanged. After we were married, I'd still write her letters: sometimes from a distant motel where I was away on a trip; sometimes from the kitchen table where I sat alone after we'd had a painful disagreement.

When tragedy struck someone close to me, a letter carried my sympathy and encouragement, talked of happier times and the things that endure beyond death. Later they'd say how much it meant to them, and I was glad I hadn't simply mailed a melancholy card.

Through the years I've written silly letters, serious letters, thoughtful letters, bland letters, poetic letters, chatty letters. When I think about it, this multiplicity of letters was probably the single most formative influence on whatever abilities I may have as a writer.

I don't write personal letters much anymore, not since my mother died two and a half years ago. Life gets hectic, the phone is easier, other people don't write — the reasons are legion. In fact, the last long letter I wrote was to my mother, just before she died. There were so many things I wanted to tell her, little things that just the two of us had shared. A letter seemed the most fitting way. It went on for pages, recalling the joys and sorrows we'd shared, the sacrifices she'd made for me, how as an adult I'd grown to appreciate her unselfishness and to recognize the pain that dogged her life. It was my testimonial to her.

She never got to read that letter. I carried it with me for three weeks, waiting for the proper moment, not wanting to intrude though daily she was slipping farther away. Finally, on a Sunday afternoon in late May, I sat beside her bed in the living room and read to her, through tears, the words I'd written. I held her hand for a squeeze of acknowledgement. There was none. The drug that fended off her pain closed her senses as well.

Late that night my mother died. At the funeral parlor the next day, before the friends and relatives came in I placed the letter in her coffin. It seemed an appropriate gesture.

ANTHONY PRETE

1 Are these essays formal or informal?

2 The essay "Uncles" is contained in the novel *Guy Lenny*. Using this pattern, create another essay entitled "Aunts."

3 Using the pattern of the essay on baseball, write an essay titled "Analysis of Basketball."

4 The essay "Subway" combines formal and informal writing. Using this model, choose another method of transportation, research it, then write the essay, incorporating your attitude toward the subject.

5 Write an editorial for your school newspaper on the subject of getting letters.

Eulogy

A eulogy is a dignified statement in honour of a dead person. It is usually given at the funeral or memorial service.

Eulogy for Jesse James

"There ain't no question 'bout it; Jesse was an outlaw, a bandit, a criminal; even those that loved him ain't got no answer to that.

But we ain't ashamed of him; I don't know why. I don't think even America's ashamed of Jesse James.

Mebbe it was because he was bold and lawless, like we all of us like to be sometimes.

Mebbe it's because we understood, a little, that he wasn't altogether to blame for what his times made him.

Mebbe it's because for ten years he licked the tar out of five states.

Or mebbe it's because he was so good at what he was doin'; I don't know.

All I do know is that he was one of the DOGGONEDEST, GOLDINGDEST, DADBLAMEDEST buckaroos that ever rode across these United States of America."

IN LOVING REMEMBRANCE OF
JESSE W. JAMES
DIED APRIL 3, 1882, AGE 34 YRS, 6 MOS., 28 DYS.
MURDERED BY A TRAITOR AND
COWARD WHOSE NAME IS NOT
WORTHY TO APPEAR HERE.

From "Jesse James"
20TH CENTURY-FOX

1 Although the language in this eulogy is informal, does the eulogy still have dignity?

2 Jesse James was a criminal. Write another eulogy for him, supposedly by a law-abiding citizen, that would appear in a local newspaper.

3 Write a eulogy for your lost childhood.

Exposition

An exposition is an explanation. The author presents facts in an organized and interesting fashion, so that the reader can easily understand the subject.

How to Tell a Tornado

Listen for noises.
If you do not live
near railroad tracks,
the freight train you hear
is not the Northern Pacific
lost in the storm:
that is a tornado
doing imitations of itself.
One of its favorite sounds
is no sound.
After the high wind, and
before the freight train,
there is a pocket of nothing:
this is when you think
everything has stopped:
do not be fooled.
Leave it all behind
except for a candle
and take to the cellar.

Afterwards
if straws are imbedded
in trees without leaves,
and your house — except
for the unbroken bathroom mirror —
has vanished
without a trace,
and you are naked
except for the right leg
of your pants,
you can safely assume
that a tornado
has gone through your life
without touching it.

HOWARD MOHR

How birds fly

Birds are adapted for flying in several ways. Their forelimbs are specialized as wings covered with flight feathers; they have powerful wing muscles, a rigid body skeleton, light hollow bones, a large heart and well-developed nervous system. There is also a system of air sacs within the bones and between the body organs which provides extra air for the increased respiration while the bird is in flight.

The wings are concave below and convex above and have a thick front (leading) edge tapering off to a thin (trailing) edge, like the wings of an aeroplane. They provide the initial lift to launch the bird in the air, and then give it forward propulsion through the air. Birds take off with a jump or short run, preferably into the wind, followed by a powerful semicircular beating of wings which produces lift on the downstroke and forward thrust on the upstroke. After gaining height the wings move with an up-and-down flapping, with the lift and thrust coming from the downbeat. The tail helps to steer and the legs are tucked out of the way so that the body is smooth and streamlined.

Waterfowl, such as ducks and swans, have greater difficulty in taking off straight from the water without a firm surface to push from. To overcome this they raise themselves with much more wing flapping. When landing, a bird slows down by widening its wings and tail and pushing its body vertically downwards to act as an air brake. A moulting bird which has lost its tail feathers lands badly because it cannot slow down quickly enough. Some birds can fly far and fast. Reliable figures are difficult to obtain, but ducks are said to fly at up to 100 kph and swifts even faster, while the peregrine falcon is said to dive at 150 kph or more. In general, the faster birds have longer and narrower wings. All birds flap their wings when they fly. A hummingbird flaps at up to 60 beats a second, but some birds save their energy by soaring and gliding. Gliding birds such as gulls and albatrosses climb or soar then gradually lose height. Vultures and some eagles soar well, using rising currents of warm air like glider pilots. Gliding birds have long narrow wings, while soarers have long broad ones.

Man's attempts to fly by imitating birds have failed, often fatally. He would need a much bigger heart, and flapping muscles that made up half his body weight, to fly in this manner.

THE PENGUIN BOOK OF THE NATURAL WORLD

Vampires

Vampires are to bodies what Ghosts are to Spirits: restless, unexpired, and needful. The Vampire possesses a body which must be clothed, housed, and fed in unique ways.

A Vampire may be recognized by the following characteristics:

He possesses an unnatural pallor, full red lips, red fires in his eyes, long, pointed canine teeth, hairy palms of hands, curving yellowish fingernails clotted with blood, and fetid breath particularly rank and corrupt.

Before feeding, a Vampire is markedly lean and gaunt. Pallor is noticeable although the lips and eyes are at all times sanguine. The skin is cold and dry. If he possesses a beard or moustache it will be faded and somewhat thinned.

After feeding, the gauntness and pallor are replaced by substantial bloat and engorgement of the entire body, the skin becoming mottled red, moist, and warm. Hair and beard will become rejuvenated, and there will be marked succulence of the lips.

Vampires are prone to dark red hair; blond Vampires are extremely rare, and bald ones almost unheard of.

If a Vampire is encountered in his coffin, he will be bloodstained about the mouth, chin, and chest as well as under the fingernails. If a vein is opened, blood will gush forth hotly; his eyes will be open at all times.

Vampires observe a strict etiquette and a technique more complex and almost more predictable than that of most night creatures.

Vampires arise from their grave, tomb, or coffin at nightfall as hunger dictates and must return there at first cockcrow. When traveling, which unsettled political conditions force them to do from time to time, they must provide themselves with a coffin or earth box containing their native soil and may cross water only when in the box, and then at great peril.

Upon arising they may assume the form of a mist, either red or white, a bat, a rodent, a dog, or they may prefer to retain their own form. Vampires can pass through doors, windows, walls, and other barriers to gain access to their victims.

When a Vampire reaches his victim he must, if the victim is a new one, be invited in the first time. For this reason they prefer as victims those who were near and dear to them in life, for the chances of receiving this crucial initial invitation are better.

BARBARA BYFIELD

1 Compare the styles of these expositions.

2 Simplify "How Birds Fly" so that it would be understandable by a primary student.

3 Write an exposition for "Ghosts" to be included in the *Book of Weird*. Use "Vampires" as your model.

4 "How to Tell a Tornado" is a satirical exposition. Create a similar poem for another disaster, such as an earthquake or volcano.

Fable

A fable is a folk tale with a moral. It teaches a lesson while telling a story. Often, animals are used to represent humans, thus protecting people's feelings.

The Glass in the Field

A short time ago some builders, working on a studio in Connecticut, left a huge square of plate glass standing upright in a field one day. A goldfinch flying swiftly across the field struck the glass and was knocked cold. When he came to he hastened to his club, where an attendant bandaged his head and gave him a stiff drink. 'What the heck happened?' asked a sea gull. 'I was flying across a meadow when all of a sudden the air crystallized on me,' said the goldfinch. The sea gull, and a hawk, and an eagle all laughed heartily. A swallow listened gravely. 'For fifteen years, fledgling and bird, I've flown this country,' said the eagle, 'and I assure you there is no such thing as air crystallizing. Water, yes; air, no.' 'You were probably struck by a hailstone,' the hawk told the goldfinch. 'Or he may have had a stroke,' said the sea gull. 'What do you think, swallow?' 'Why, I — I think maybe the air crystallized on him,' said the swallow. The large birds laughed so loudly that the goldfinch became annoyed and bet them each a dozen worms that they couldn't follow the course he had flown across the field without encountering the hardened atmosphere. They all took his bet; the swallow went along to watch. The sea gull, the eagle, and the hawk decided to fly together over the route the goldfinch indicated. 'You come, too,' they said to the swallow. 'I — I — well no,' said the swallow. 'I don't think I will.' So the three large birds took off together and they hit the glass together and they were all knocked cold.

Moral: He who hesitates is sometimes saved.

JAMES THURBER

The Swan

The swan arched his supple neck towards the water and gazed at his reflection for a long time.

He understood the reason for his weariness and for the cold that gripped his body, making him tremble as though it were winter. With absolute certainty, he knew that his hour had come and that he must prepare for death.

His feathers were still as white as they had been on the first day of his life. Seasons and years had passed without a blemish appearing on his snowy plumage. He could go now, and his life would end in beauty.

Straightening his beautiful neck, he swam slowly and majestically beneath a willow, where he had been accustomed to rest in the hot weather. It was already evening, and the sunset was touching the water of the lake with crimson and violet.

And in the great silence that was falling all around, the swan began to sing.

Never before had he found notes so full of love for all of nature, for the beauty of the heavens, the water and the earth. His sweet song rang through the air, scarcely tinged with melancholy, until, softly, softly, it faded with the last traces of light on the horizon.

"It is the swan," said the fishes, the birds, and all the beasts of woodland and meadow. Touched to the heart, they said: "The swan is dying."

LEONARDO DA VINCI

The Bear and the Crow

The Bear was on his way to town. He was dressed in his finest coat and vest. He was wearing his best derby hat and his shiniest shoes. "How grand I look," said the Bear to himself. "The townsfolk will be impressed. My clothes are at the height of fashion."

"Forgive me for listening," said a Crow, who was sitting on the branch of a tree, "but I must disagree. Your clothes are *not* at the height of fashion. I have just flown in from town. I can tell you exactly how the gentlemen are dressed there."

"Do tell me!" cried the Bear. "I am so eager to wear the most proper attire!"

are covering themselves with bed sheets. They are not wearing shoes. They are putting paper bags on their feet."

"Oh, dear," cried the Bear, "my clothes are completely wrong!"

The Bear hurried home. He took off his coat and vest and hat and shoes. He put a frying pan on his head. He wrapped himself in a bed sheet. He stuffed his feet into large paper bags and rushed off toward the town.

When the Bear arrived on Main Street, the people giggled and smirked and pointed their fingers.

"What a ridiculous Bear!" they said.

The embarrassed Bear turned around and ran home. On the way he met the Crow again.

"Crow, you did not tell me the truth!" cried the Bear.

"I told you many things," said the Crow, as he flew out of the tree, "but never once did I tell you that I was telling the truth!"

Even though the Crow was high in the sky, the Bear could still hear the shrill sound of his cackling laughter.

When the need is strong, there are those who will believe anything.

ARNOLD LOBEL

1 What lessons are being taught in these fables?

2 Retell the fable "The Swan" as a story, using just the facts.

3 Retell "The Glass in the Field" as a poem.

4 Using the moral in "The Bear and the Crow," create another fable.

"This year," said the Crow, "the gentlemen are not wearing hats. They all have frying pans on their heads. They are not wearing coats and vests. They

Fairy tale

The fairy tale is part of folklore. The story may be simple, but its meanings are deep. Fairy tales concern the adventures of characters caught in the mysterious or supernatural world.

The Princess and the Peas

There lived, once upon a time, a Prince, and he wished to marry a Princess, but then she must be really and truly a Princess. So he travelled over the whole world to find one; but there was always something or other to prevent his being successful. Princesses he found in plenty, but he never could make out if they were real Princesses; for sometimes one thing and sometimes another appeared to him not quite right about the ladies. So at last he returned home quite cast down; for he wanted so very much to have a real Princess for a wife.

One evening, a dreadful storm was gathering; it thundered and lightened, and the rain poured down from heaven in torrents; it was, too, as dark as pitch. Suddenly a loud knocking was heard at the town-gates; and the old King, the Prince's father, went out himself to see who was there.

It was a Princess that stood at the gate; but, Lord bless me! what a figure she was from the rain! The water ran down from her hair, and her dress was dripping wet and stuck quite close to her body. She said she was a real Princess.

'We'll soon see that,' thought the old Queen Dowager: however, she said not a word, but went into the bed-room, took out all the bedding, and laid three small peas on the bottom of the bedstead. Then she took, first, twenty mattresses, and laid them one upon the other on the three peas, and then she took twenty feather-beds more, and put these again a-top of the mattresses.

This was the bed the Princess was to sleep in.

The next morning she asked her if she had had a good night.

'Oh, no! a horrid night!' said the Princess. 'I was hardly able to close my eyes the whole night! Heaven knows what was in my bed, but there was a something hard under me, and my whole body is black and blue with bruises! I can't tell you what I've suffered!'

Then they knew that the lady they had lodged was a real Princess, since she had felt the three small peas through twenty mattresses and twenty feather-beds; for it was quite impossible for any one but a true Princess to be so tender.

So the Prince married her; for he was now convinced that he had a real Princess for his wife. The three peas were deposited in the Museum, where they are still to be seen; that is to say, if they have not been lost.

Now was not that a lady of exquisite feeling?

IONA AND PETER OPIE

Rapunzel, Rapunzel

Rapunzel, Rapunzel,
Let down your golden hair
As far as to the top step
Of the stone stair,

The stone stair, Rapunzel,
That goes on down forever.
There is no coming up again,
Ever, ever, ever.

Rapunzel, Rapunzel,
Nevertheless I came.
For love of you I climbed it.
Here then I am.

Rapunzel, Rapunzel,
Be kind to me at last.
Let down your long and golden hair —
But haste, Rapunzel, haste!

MARK VAN DOREN

The Horse that had a Flat Tire

Once upon a valley
there came down
from some goldenblue mountains
a handsome young prince
who was riding
a dawncolored horse
named Lordsburg.

    I love you
    You're my breathing castle
    Gentle so gentle
    We'll live forever

In the valley
there was a beautiful maiden
whom the prince
drifted into love with
like a New Mexico made from
apple thunder and long
glass beds.

    I love you
    You're my breathing castle
    Gentle so gentle
    We'll live forever

The prince enchanted
the maiden
and they rode off
on the dawncolored horse
named Lordsburg
toward the goldenblue mountains.

    I love you
    You're my breathing castle
    Gentle so gentle
    We'll live forever

They would have lived
happily ever after
if the horse hadn't had
a flat tire
in front of a dragon's
house.

RICHARD BRAUTIGAN

1 How do these fairy tales fit the above definition?

2 Retell "The Princess and the Peas" from the viewpoint of the mother assessing her future daughter-in-law.

3 Write the sequel to the fairy tale "The Horse that had a Flat Tire."

4 A prince has written to a newspaper columnist complaining that his tests to find a princess have failed. He requests the true test. Write the columnist's response.

5 Choose a folk tale and retell it as a poem, using "Rapunzel, Rapunzel" as a model.

Fantasy

Fantasy takes place in an unreal world. Unlike science fiction, fantasy is based purely on the author's imagination — it does not depend on scientific truth. Fantasy concerns unreal and incredible characters.

A Hobbit-hole

In a hole in the ground there lived a hobbit. Not a nasty, dirty, wet hole, filled with the ends of worms and an oozy smell, nor yet a dry, bare, sandy hole with nothing in it to sit down on or to eat: it was a hobbit-hole, and that means comfort.

It had a perfectly round door like a porthole, painted green, with a shiny yellow brass knob in the exact middle. The door opened on to a tube-shaped hall like a tunnel: a very comfortable tunnel without smoke, with panelled walls, and floors tiled and carpeted, provided with polished chairs, and lots and lots of pegs for hats and coats — the hobbit was fond of visitors. The tunnel wound on and on, going fairly but not quite straight into the side of the hill — The Hill, as all the people for a distance round called it — and many little round doors opened out of it, first on one side and then on another. No going upstairs for the hobbit: bedrooms, bath-rooms, cellars, pantries (lots of these), wardrobes (he had whole rooms devoted to clothes), kitchens, dining-rooms, all were on the same floor, and indeed on the same passage. The best rooms were all on the lefthand side (going in), for these were the only ones to have windows, deep-set round windows looking over his garden, and meadows beyond, sloping down to the river.

This hobbit was a very well-to-do hobbit, and his name was Baggins. The Bagginses had lived in the neighbourhood of The Hill for time out of mind, and people considered them very respectable, not only because most of them were rich, but also because they never had any adventures or did anything unexpected: you could tell what a Baggins would say on any question without the bother of asking him. This is a story of how a Baggins had an adventure, and found himself doing and saying things altogether unexpected. He may have lost the neighbours' respect, but he gained — well, you will see whether he gained anything in the end.

The mother of our particular hobbit — what is a hobbit? I suppose hobbits need some description nowadays, since they have become rare and shy of the Big People, as they call us. They are (or were) a little people, about half our height, and smaller than the bearded Dwarves. Hobbits have no beards. There is little or no magic about them, except the ordinary everyday sort which helps them to disappear quietly and quickly when large stupid folk like you and me come blundering along, making a noise like elephants which they can hear a mile off. They are inclined to be fat in the stomach; they dress in bright colours (chiefly green and yellow); wear no shoes, because their feet grow natural leathery soles and thick warm brown hair like the stuff on their heads (which is curly); have long clever brown fingers, good-natured faces, and laugh deep fruity laughs (especially after dinner, which they have twice a day when they can get it). Now you know enough to go on with. As I was saying, the mother of this hobbit — of Bilbo Baggins, that is — was the fabulous Belladonna Took, one of the three remarkable daughters of the Old Took, head of the hobbits who lived across The Water, the small river that ran at the foot of The Hill. It was often said (in other families) that long ago one of the Took ancestors must have taken a fairy wife. That was, of course, absurd, but certainly there was still something not entirely hobbitlike about them, and once in a while members of the Took-clan would go and have adventures. They discreetly disappeared, and the family hushed it up; but the fact remained that the Tooks were not as respectable as the Bagginses, though they were undoubtedly richer.

Not that Belladonna Took ever had any adventures after she became Mrs. Bungo Baggins. Bungo, that was Bilbo's father, built the most luxurious hobbit-hole for her (and partly with her money) that was to be found either under The Hill or over The Hill or across The Water, and there they remained to the end of their days. Still it is probable that Bilbo, her only son, although he looked and behaved exactly like a second edition of his solid and comfortable father, got something a bit queer in his make-up from the Took side, something that only waited for a chance to come out. The chance never arrived, until Bilbo Baggins was grown up, being about fifty years old or so, and living in the beautiful hobbit-hole built by his father, which I have just described for you, until he had in fact apparently settled down immovably.

J. R. R. TOLKIEN

Dragonsong

JACKET BLURB

For long periods of time, at intervals of two hundred years or so, the people of Pern had to contend with falls of threadlike spores, which consumed all living matter. To counteract this menace, men developed huge dragons, capable of breathing out great tongues of fire that destroyed the Threads. They and their dragonriders protected the planet during Threadfall, while all other people stayed safely in their cavelike Holds.

It was not growing up in a time of Threadfall that made Menolly unhappy, however. It was the fact that she loved music and wanted to be a Harper, though her father believed it was a disgrace for a woman even to think of such. Finally, he would not even allow her to sing with the whole group, for fear her ambition would become known.

Menolly lived with the situation as long as she could; then finally she had no choice but to run away. Being without music was worse than the prospect of being outside during Threadfall.

Menolly was resourceful, and she was kind, two attributes that did her good service when she came upon a group of fire lizards, small relations of the huge dragons of Pern. It was the friendship of nine of these creatures, and the discovery that they could be taught to sing, that brought adventure, challenge, and a new directive to Menolly's life.

1 How are these fantasy selections different from science fiction?

2 Imagine that you are a hobbit writing an encyclopedia. Write the entry for "Big People."

3 "Menolly finally had no choice but to run away." Write the episode that describes Menolly's first few days outside the cave during Threadfall.

4 Write an essay in defence of fantasy.

Folklore

Folklore consists of the traditional beliefs of a people. Much of folklore has been passed down orally in sayings, proverbs, and superstitions.

The Zoo in Your Dreams

Dream of a crocodile, wake to danger.
  Dream of a lobster and wake to wealth.
Dream of a dog and you'll meet a stranger.
  Dream of a frog and you'll know good health.

Dream of a squirrel — your hopes mount higher.
  Dream of an eagle and grow to fame.
Dream of a wolf and you'll meet a liar.
  (Dream mice or monkeys for much the same.)

Dream of a bear and it's odds agin' you.
  Dream of a bull and a rival's there.
Dream of a swan and pleasure will win you.
  Dream of a shark and you'll know despair.

        Dream of beetles and worries arise.
        Dream of a fish for a nice surprise.

PETER DICKINSON

Proverbs and superstitions

When the cat wears gloves she can't catch any mice.

A lie one mustn't say — some truths you shouldn't say.

He's such a thief, he'll steal the crack of your whip if you don't look.

You must never show half-completed work to a fool.

Don't spit into the well — you might drink from it later.

TRADITIONAL

Spells

I dance and dance without any feet —
This is the spell of the ripening wheat.

With never a tongue I've a tale to tell —
This is the meadow-grasses' spell.

I give you health without any fee —
This is the spell of the apple-tree.

I rhyme and riddle without any book —
This is the spell of the bubbling brook.

Without any legs I run for ever —
This is the spell of the mighty river.

I fall for ever and not at all —
This is the spell of the waterfall.

Without a voice I roar aloud —
This is the spell of the thunder-cloud.

No button or seam has my white coat —
This is the spell of the leaping goat.

I can cheat strangers with never a word —
This is the spell of the cuckoo-bird.

We have tongues in plenty but speak no
    names —
This is the spell of the fiery flames.

The creaking door has a spell to riddle —
I play a tune without any fiddle.

JAMES REEVES

Bad Luck Signs

To look into a mirror at night.

To draw the window blinds before lighting the lamps.

To spill salt — the evil may be counteracted by burning the salt.

To boast of good health — you will be sure to be ill soon after.

To take either a cat or a broom along when moving from one house to another.

Collected by EDITH FOWKE

Death Signs

Two forks on a table.

The hooting of an owl near a house.

When a wild bird enters an occupied house.

If a cock crows before ten o'clock.

The last person mentioned by a dying person will be the next to die.

Collected by EDITH FOWKE

The Old Men Admiring Themselves in the Water

I heard the old, old men say,
'Everything alters,
And one by one we drop away.'
They had hands like claws, and their knees
Were twisted like the old thorn-trees
By the waters.
I heard the old, old men say,
'All that's beautiful drifts away
Like the waters.'

W. B. YEATS

1 What can you learn about people from these selections of folklore?

2 What omens does society today use to forecast bad luck?

3 Retell as a folk tale one of the dreams in "The Zoo in Your Dreams."

4 Rewrite these proverbs and superstitions as modern rules for living.

5 Choose one of these proverbs. Create a poem from it, using "The Old Men Admiring Themselves in the Water as a pattern."

Folk song

Traditionally, folk songs were preserved and passed on by minstrels and troubadors. Folk songs told stories, raised people's spirits, helped recall the past, or taught lessons. Modern composers create folk songs by imitating songs from the past.

Hard, Hard Times

1. So now I'm intending to sing you a song
    About the poor people, how they get along.
    They start in the spring and they work till the fall,
    And when they clew up they have nothing at all,

CHORUS:
    And it's hard, hard times.

2. *You start with the jigger the first in the spring,*
    And across the gunnel you'll make the lines sing;
    Perhaps lose your jigger, get froze with the cold,
    Now that's the first starting of going in the hole . . .

3. It's out with the traps and the trawls too likewise,
   Perhaps get a kentle, a good sign for the voyage.
   You'll feel up in spirits and work with a will —
   Next morning adrift, you've gone in the hole still . . .

4. When so much is caught and then put out to dry
   The next is the trouble to keep off the flies.
   It's buzz all around, more trouble for you —
   Then out shines the sun and it's split right in two . . .

5. Then here comes the schooners — go get your supplies;
   A good price this summer — just make it good, b'ys.
   Seven for the large fish and five for the small,
   Pick out your West Indies and wait till the fall . . .

6. Then here comes the carpenter, he will build you a house:
   He will build it so snug that you'll scarce see a mouse.
   There'll be leaks in the roof, there'll be holes in the floor,
   The chimney will smoke, and it's open the door . . .

7. The next comes the doctor, the worst of them all,
   Saying, 'What is the matter with you all the fall?'
   He says he will cure you of all your disease —
   When he gets all your money, you can die if you please . . .

8. But never mind, friends, let us work with a will.
   When we finish down here we'll be hauled on the hill,
   And there they will lay us down deep in the cold —
   When all here is finished, you're still in the hole . . .

Collected by EDITH FOWKE

1 Why has this song survived from the past?
2 Add a stanza to this song explaining the student's life.
3 Research what contemporary songs say about work and write a brief essay.
4 Produce a transcript from an interview with a worker.

Folk tale

A folk tale is a story that has been handed down by word of mouth from generation to generation. Folk tales are simple stories about simple people. Yet, through these stories, traditions have survived.

Axe Porridge

An old soldier was once on his way home for his leave, and he was tired and hungry. He reached a village and he rapped at the first hut.

'Let a traveller in for the night,' said he.

The door was opened by an old woman.

'Come in, soldier,' she offered.

'Have you a bite of food for a hungry man, good dame?' the soldier asked.

Now the old woman had plenty of everything, but she was stingy and pretended to be very poor.

'Ah, me, I've had nothing to eat myself today, dear heart, there is nothing in the house,' she wailed.

'Well, if you've nothing, you've nothing,' the soldier said. Then, noticing an axe without a handle under the bench: 'If there's nothing else, we could make porridge out of that axe.'

The old woman raised both hands in astonishment.

'Axe porridge? Who ever heard the like!'

'I'll show you how to make it. Just give me a pot.'

The old woman brought a pot, and the soldier washed the axe, put it in the pot, and filling the pot with water, placed it on the fire.

The soldier got out a spoon and stirred the water and then tasted it.

'It will soon be ready,' said he. 'A pity there's no salt.'

'Oh, I have salt. Here, take some.'

The soldier put some salt in the pot and then tried the water again.

'If we could just add a handful of groats to it,' said he.

The old woman brought a small bag of groats from the pantry.

'Here, add as much as you need,' said she.

The soldier went on with his cooking, stirring the meal from time to time and tasting it. And the old woman watched, and could not tear her eyes away.

'Oh, how tasty this porridge is!' the soldier said, trying a spoonful. 'With a bit of butter there would be nothing more delicious.'

The old woman found some butter too, and they buttered the porridge.

'Now get a spoon, good dame, and let us eat!' the soldier said.

They began eating the porridge and praising it.

'I never thought axe porridge could taste so good!' the old woman marvelled.

And the soldier ate, and laughed up his sleeve.

TRADITIONAL RUSSIAN

Henny Penny

HENNY PENNY!
THE SKY IS FALLING!
THE SKY IS FALLING!

DUCKY LUCKY!
THE SKY IS FALLING!
THE SKY IS FALLING!

TURKEY LURKEY!
THE SKY IS FALLING!
THE SKY IS FALLING!

You wouldn't happen to know who comes after Turkey Lurkey?

BOYNTON

The Prince and the Flea

There was once a prince who was tormented by a flea. He finally caught it under his shirt.

'Do not kill me!' said the flea. 'The harm I have done you is very small!'

'All the harm that was in your power to do, you did!' replied the prince, and squashed him to death.

TRADITIONAL ARMENIAN

Earth-Moon

Once upon a time there was a person
He was walking along
He met the full burning moon
Rolling slowly towards him
Crushing the stones and houses by the wayside.
He shut his eyes from the glare.
He drew his dagger
And stabbed and stabbed and stabbed.
The cry that quit the moon's wounds
Circled the earth.
The moon shrank, like a punctured airship,
Shrank, shrank, smaller, smaller,
Till it was nothing
But a silk handkerchief, torn,
And wet as with tears.
The person picked it up. He walked on
Into moonless night
Carrying this strange trophy.

TED HUGHES

1 Do these selections follow the folk tale pattern?

2 Turn "Axe Porridge" into a shooting script for an animated film.

3 The tale "The Prince and the Flea" represents the use of symbolism. Retell the tale as a brief essay explaining the hidden, symbolic meaning of the flea.

4 This telling of "Henny Penny" contains a surprise ending. Choose another folk tale and retell it in this style.

5 "Earth-Moon" is a modern poem that uses the style of the folk tale. Recreate the poem as a science fiction short story.

Found poetry

Found poetry does not originate as poetry. The poet finds an interesting selection or excerpt and arranges the words or sentences into poetic form.

Canadian Indian Place Names

Bella Bella, Bella Coola,
Athabaska, Iroquois;
Mesilinka, Osilinka,
Mississauga, Missisquois.
Chippewa, Chippawa,
Nottawasaga;
Oshawa, Ottawa,
Nassagaweya;
Malagash, Matchedash,
Shubenacadie;
Couchiching, Nipissing,
Scubenacadie.
Shickshock
Yahk
Quaw!

MEGUIDO ZOLA

Ice Cream Cone

Flour, cereal, sugar, starch,
vegetable shortening,
salt, protein, gum leavening,
propylene glycol.
Certified colors, artificial flavors.
Chocolate coating containing
cocoa, vegetable oil (containing
an emulsifier and tenox 2
less than .05%).
Tenox 2
is an antioxident containing
butylated hydroxyanisole,
propyl gallate, citric acid,
propylene glycol.

RONALD GROSS

1 What is the origin of each of these selections? What makes them poetry?

2 Choose a list of ingredients similar to "Ice Cream Cone." Re-arrange it into a form so that the new-found poem makes a statement.

3 Using the street names in your neighbourhood, re-arrange them in a rhythmic pattern using "Canadian Indian Place Names" as a model.

4 Write an advertisement based on the information in "Ice Cream Cone."

Free verse

Grizzly at Night

may
one month before the indian paintbrush
  flourishes
the mist descends the cold mountain

hands deeply pocketed
i walk home from a friend's place
a fresh loaf of bread
warm against my chest

a grizzly looms up from dark deadwoods ahead
  of me
stops
and shakes the frost from his mane
then looking my way sniffs a sweet aroma
nods his voluminous head
as if to say
"what are you carrying so carefully
beneath your coat
pilgrim?"

remembering her gentle white hands
braiding the bread
i silently answer
"something to keep me warm brother
warm against the cold
this side of the river"

ANDREW SUKNASKI

The projectionist's nightmare

This is the projectionist's nightmare:
A bird finds its way into the cinema,
finds the beam, flies down it,
smashes into a screen depicting a garden,
a sunset and two people being nice to each
  other.
Real blood, real intestines, slither down
the likeness of a tree.
'This is no good,' screams the audience,
'This is not what we came to see.'

BRIAN PATTEN

1 How do these poems differ from prose?

2 What could startle you at night in your neighbourhood? Using the pattern of "Grizzly at Night," write a similar poem about your reactions.

3 What if the characters in "The Projectionist's Nightmare" suddenly saw the bird? Write a free-verse poem describing their reactions.

4 Choose one of these poems. You have been part of the experiences described. Write the dialogue that would occur when you tried to explain to someone what you had seen.

A ghost story is a mixture of the supernatural and the mysterious. The storyteller, whether in writing or in speech, attempts to create a mood and atmosphere that help the audience accept the possibility that ghosts exist.

Milk Bottles

This happened many years ago in a small country village in Alabama.

One day the storekeeper looked up and saw a pale young woman in a gray dress standing at the counter.

"What can I do for you, ma'am?" he said.

She did not answer, but pointed to a bottle of milk. The storekeeper handed it to her, and without a word she walked quickly out of the store and down the main street of the town.

The next day she came back.

"What will you have today, ma'am?" the store-keeper asked.

The young woman in gray pointed to a bottle of milk.

Again the storekeeper handed it to her. And once again the woman took the milk and hurried away without saying a word.

That night the storekeeper told his neighbors about the strange young woman in gray with the sad, pale face who came every day for milk and walked away without thanks or payment, in silence.

So the next day when the woman in gray appeared and again walked away with the milk without speaking, two or three of the villagers followed her.

She walked swiftly down the main street of the town. The men were amazed that they almost had to run to keep sight of her.

She passed the school; she passed the church; she kept right on through the little town up the hill to the graveyard.

She passed swiftly in among the graves and stones and trees, seemed to stop for a minute — and then was gone.

The followers stood quietly beside the grave where the slender gray figure had seemed to pause. It was the new-made grave of a young mother and her baby daughter who had died three days ago of a fever. In fact, she had died just one day before she first came into the store for milk.

It all seemed so strange and mysterious that the villagers thought they ought to investigate. So they came back with shovels and soon unearthed the young mother's coffin.

Then, while they were moving the coffin, they heard — or thought they heard — a tiny muffled wail.

They listened.

They heard it again — the feeble little cry of a baby.

Quickly they opened the coffin.

Yes. Here was the frail young mother in gray who had come for the milk. And in her arms lay a baby girl — ill and weak, but *alive*.

Beside her lay the empty milk bottles.

One of the men took the baby home to his wife, and the little life was saved.

No one ever saw the young mother in gray again. She had accomplished her task. She had saved her baby girl.

Now she could rest.

MARIA LEACH

1 What techniques does the author use to create the ghostlike atmosphere?

2 Re-tell this ghost story in the first person, as if you were one of the people who followed the woman in the grey dress.

3 Truth is stranger than fiction. What stories have you heard people tell that involved the supernatural? Re-tell one of these stories as a ghost story.

4 Write a short essay in which you state your viewpoint on the existence of ghosts.

Gothic writing

The elements of gothic writing are magic, mystery, medieval castles, strange unexpected happenings, horrors, and an atmosphere of terror.

Nurse J. Rosebeetle

tilted her employer out of a wheelchair
and over a cliff
at Sludgemouth in 1898.

"Nurse J. Rosebeetle" by Edward Gorey © 1980 by Edward Gorey. Reprinted from *Dancing Cats and Neglected Murderesses* by permission of Workman Publishing Co., Inc., N.Y.

The Werewolf

The full moon glows, foreboding,
and I quake from head to feet
for this night I know, in the town below,
the werewolf prowls the street.

He stalks with stealth and cunning
in his search for a soul to eat.
With matted hair and jaws that tear,
the werewolf prowls the street.

His face is filled with fury
as his brain cries out for meat,
and oh his prey shall not see day
for the werewolf prowls the street.

So I shake beneath my covers
and I shiver in my sheet
and I cower in my bed with a pillow on my
    head,
as the werewolf prowls the street.

JACK PRELUTSKY

The Thing in the Cellar

It was a large cellar, entirely out of proportion to the house above it. The owner admitted that it was probably built for a distinctly different kind of structure from the one which rose above it. Probably the first house had been burned, and poverty had caused a diminution of the dwelling erected to take its place.

A winding stone stairway connected the cellar with the kitchen. Around the base of this series of steps successive owners of the house had placed their firewood, winter vegetables, and junk. The junk had gradually been pushed back till it rose, head high, in a barricade of uselessness. What was back of that barricade no one knew and no one cared. For some hundreds of years no one had crossed it to penetrate to the black reaches of the cellar behind.

At the top of the steps, separating the kitchen from the cellar, was a stout oaken door. This door was, in a way, as peculiar and out of relation to the rest of the house as the cellar. It was a strange kind of door to find in a modern house, and certainly a most unusual door to find in the inside of the house — thick, stoutly built, dexterously rabbeted together, with huge wrought-iron hinges, and a lock that looked as though it came from Castle Despair. Separating a house from the outside world, such a door would be excusable; swinging between kitchen and cellar, it seemed peculiarly inappropriate.

From the earliest months of his life Tommy Tucker seemed unhappy in the kitchen.

DAVID H. KELLER

1 How do these selections fit the definition of gothic writing?

2 Expand the story of Nurse J. Rosebeetle into a gothic tale.

3 The moon disappears and daylight comes. What are the tell-tale signs that the werewolf's wife notices when he returns home? Write this chapter in the gothic tale.

4 "The Thing in the Cellar" is the beginning of a gothic tale. Finish the story, using such elements as long underground passages, trap doors, dark stairways, and doors that slam unexpectedly.

Haiku

Haiku is a poem of seventeen syllables. Formal Japanese haiku are based on three unrhymed lines of five, seven, and five syllables respectively. Using the senses, the poet observes and records his or her experiences in exact language.

The song of the bird!
But the plum-tree in the grove
Is not yet blooming.

ISSA

The wild cherry:
Stones also are singing their songs
In the valley stream.

ONITSURA

A fire-fly flitted by:
"Look" I almost said, —
But I was alone.

TAIGI

White chrysanthemums!
Where is there a color
So happy, so gracious?

BUSON

1 You are the poet. Write a haiku describing one of the experiences from another point of view.

2 Write the first two lines of a haiku. Exchange your unfinished poem with another student and finish his or her poem. Try to collect several endings for each poem. Study them for the effects created.

3 Using a slogan or jingle from an advertisement, change it into a haiku.

Historical fiction

Historical fiction is a picture in words of a bygone age. Often, an author of historical fiction will incorporate actual events or characters into his fictional account of the time. The author may alter the facts, however, in order to create a story.

Mirror, Mirror

Between Glass House Yard and Shoemaker's Row lies Friers Street, where Mr. Paris's premises occupy a commanding position on a corner. In the gloom of the November evening his shop window flares out extravagantly, as platoons of candles execute various dancing manoeuvres in flawless unison. On closer inspection, however, they turn out to be a single candle reflected in a cunning display of looking-glasses. Mr. Paris is a master carver of mirror-frames; golden boys and golden grapes cluster round the silver mirrors and seem to invite, with dimpled arms outstretched, the passer-by to pause and contemplate himself.

Inside, in the dining parlour, the family are sitting down to supper: Mr. and Mrs. Paris — a handsome couple who will be middle-aged when it suits them — Miss Lucinda, their young daughter, and Nightingale, the new apprentice.

Nightingale has not long arrived. He has scarcely had time to wash himself before sitting down to table. All day he has been tramping the streets with his father, a Hertfordshire joiner, and gaping at the multitudinous sights of the town. All in all, it has been a solemn day, what with the many unspoken leave-takings between father and son, the looks over the tops of toasting tankards of ale, the deep pressings of hands, the sentences begun and left half finished as the same melancholy thought strikes them both . . .

They have never before been parted; or at least, not for more than a day. But now the inevitable time has come. Ten pounds has been paid for the apprenticeship and Daniel Nightingale is to embark alone on the great voyage of life . . . as the village parson had been pleased to put it. Like all such voyages, it is to be seven years long, and the only provisions that the father might properly give his son to take with him have been the wise precepts he himself has treasured up and written down from his own seven years of apprenticeship.

Never come between your master and mistress . . .

Nightingale looks up the table at Mr. Paris and then down the table at Mrs. Paris; the husband and wife gaze at one another with identical smiles, as if each is the reflection of the other's heart.

Carry no tales or gossip between master and mistress, nor chatter with the servants of their private affairs . . .

A greasy girl comes in with a dish of mutton and a carving knife. She puts them both on the table with a glance at Nightingale that makes his blood run cold.

Look upon your master as another parent to you . . .

Nightingale catches Mr. Paris's eye, but finds it altogether too slippery to hold. Mournfully he remembers his own parent; only a few hours ago he was 'Daniel, boy . . . Dan, dear . . .' Now that fond distinction has been shorn away and he is plain 'Nightingale'.

Perhaps now that I'm just a Nightingale, he thinks as a plate is set before him, I ought to sing for my supper? He smiles to himself, not having thought of many jokes before, wit in Hertfordshire being as thin on the ground as turnips are thick. Mr. and Mrs. Paris continue with their own smiles and the table presents an amiable aspect . . . with the exception of Miss Lucinda, the master's pretty daughter. She dislikes the new apprentice for no better reason than that he has failed to recognize her as the queen of the household. She knows it is every apprentice's ambition to wed his master's daughter and she cannot endure the notion of being a rung in someone else's ladder to the sky. She is not much beyond fourteen, with fair hair, fair skin and a general brilliancy about her that suggests she has caught some shining complaint from her father's wares.

'I hope and trust, Master Nightingale,' says Mr. Paris, never taking his eyes off his wife, 'that at the end of your seven years we will all be as contented and smiling as we are now?'

The apprentice, caught with his mouth full, nods politely. At the same time, mournful thoughts of the day return. Seven years; seven long years . . .

After the meal, Mr. Paris rises and shows Nightingale where he is to sleep. According to usage, the apprentice's bed is made up under the counter in the front room that serves as showroom and shop; thus if dreams come, they are more likely than not to be dreams arising from the day's work, so no time will be wasted. Mr. Paris bids Nightingale goodnight and leaves him with a wax candle which he must be sparing with, as it is to last him for a week.

The apprentice mumbles his thanks and, when he is alone, prepares to say his nightly prayers. He is scarcely on his knees before the door opens abruptly and startles him. His master's daughter stands in the doorway. He has no time to observe her before she calls out:

'Nightingale! Catch!'

She tosses something towards him that glitters in the candlelight like a speeding star. The apprentice is too surprised to do more than put out a hand that just touches the object before it falls with a crash to the ground. It is, or, rather, was, a looking-glass. Now it lies on the floor, shattered into silver knives and slices. Miss Lucinda smiles.

'You've broken a mirror, Nightingale. That means seven years' bad luck.'

• • •

LEON GARFIELD

1 Leon Garfield became famous as a writer of stories for young people that were set in the eighteenth century. Why might he have chosen that time?

2 This story is about becoming an apprentice in the eighteenth century. You are a journalist investigating the conditions of apprentices; you interview Nightingale. Write the transcript of the interview.

3 Did Nightingale have seven years of bad luck? Write the final event in the story of this apprentice.

Hymn

Glorious It Is

Glorious it is to see
The caribou flocking down from the forests
And beginning
Their wanderings to the north.
Timidly they watch
For the pitfalls of man.
Glorious it is to see
The great herds from the forests
Spreading out over plains of white.
Glorious to see.

Glorious it is to see
Early summer's short-haired caribou
Beginning to wander.
Glorious to see them trot
To and fro
Across the promontories,
Seeking a crossing place.

Glorious it is
To see the great musk oxen
Gathering in herds.
The little dogs they watch for
When they gather in herds.
Glorious to see.

. . .

Glorious it is
To see long-haired winter caribou
Returning to the forests.
Fearfully they watch
For the little people,
While the herd follows the ebb-mark of the sea
With a storm of clattering hooves.
Glorious it is
When wandering time is come.

COPPER ESKIMO

Translated by KNUD RASMUSSEN

Hymn to the Sun

Beautiful you rise upon the horizon of heaven,
O living sun, you have existed since the
    beginning of things . . .
The whole world is filled with your loveliness.
You are the god Ra, and you have brought every
    land under your yoke,
Bound them in with the force of your love.
You are far away, yet your beams flood down
    upon the earth.
You shine upon the faces of men,
And no one is able to fathom the mystery of
    your coming.

Translated by J. E. MANCHIP WHITE

1 What are the participants celebrating in these two hymns?

2 Using the pattern of "Hymn to the Sun," write another hymn for modern sun-worshippers.

3 In your life, what things do you see that you wish to celebrate in a hymn?

4 As a class, compose the hymn that represents your country. This hymn is to be sung at the next Olympic Games.

An interview is the record of a conversation between an interviewer and the subject. The interviewer's purpose is to present to the reader a full picture of the subject: the facts about his or her life, views on various issues, and hopes for the future.

James Houston

James Houston served in the Toronto Scottish Regiment in the Second World War. Afterwards he studied art in France and it was following his return to Canada, on a sketching trip, that he first saw the Arctic. He stayed 12 years. The first nine were spent as a northern service officer, and then he was appointed civil administrator of West Baffin Island. He played a major role in introducing Inuit art to the outside world, and his Arctic experiences have, so far, been the inspiration for many sculptures, engravings, and drawings, as well as 11 adult and children's books. His latest novel is *Spirit Wrestler* (M & S). Houston now divides his time between a Rhode Island farm and a home in the Queen Charlotte Islands, spending half a year in each place. He spoke to Phil Surguy [of the periodical *Books in Canada*] while on a recent visit to Toronto:

Books in Canada: *Can you think of an initial or primary experience with the Inuit that you are now reliving or recreating in your novels, particularly* The White Dawn *and* Spirit Wrestler?

Houston: I'm especially interested in contact between native people and newcomers, cultural clashes between the two. We have a remarkable thing; we always feel that we are well-educated and that other people are not. But look at an Inuit hunter. He's using all the careful, specialized education that had been given to him down through his grandfathers for 5000 years in a direct line, none of this classroom stuff of 40 pupils, but one-to-one. Yet somehow we can sit around in supreme confidence, and feel that we are wonderful, masterful people and all other people are just poor simple people who have not taken calculation.

BiC: *Do you ever feel self-conscious about writing from an Eskimo point of view?*

Houston: Perhaps I should. But the thing about a writer is I do think he's got to be a bit bold. I had the luck to live with those people for a long time. They're godfathers to my children and I'm godfather to their children and we have a very close, family relationship. My son is still in the Arctic, working and doing things. So we have an ongoing, close connection with the Inuit world.

BiC: *In* Spirit Wrestler *you come within a hair's breadth of actually saying that the magic that lives in the Inuit world and Inuit imagination is real.*

Houston: Well, I do.

BiC: *Is* it *real?*

Houston: Yes, I think it's real. I find that hard to say. Part of me says it cannot be, but another part of me says, how could it possibly be like that if it wasn't so? I did see a man weaving on a snow bench inside an igloo — almost 30 years ago — and they were using an accordion instead of a drum for a shamanistic seance, and that man, when I least expected it (and I was as close as I am to you) he lunged onto a harpoon and drove it straight through his chest and it came out his back. Blood gushed from his mouth and people were screaming and I looked at him and I thought, what am I going to write in the government monthly report about *this*? I was horrified. I thought he was dead. This man's just committed suicide right before my eyes. Two men grabbed him under the arms and dragged him out of the snow house. I started out after them, just expecting to see him lying there dead and figuring out what I was going to do about it. I was the coroner in the area as well. But as I went out he was on his way back in. There was lots of blood all over him. He pulled up his parka in front and back, and there were big holes in it, but no hole in his chest, and he said, "I'm not dead."

BiC: *There's a scene in* Spirit Wrestler *where Morgan, the anthropologist, is trying to roll his kayak and he's grabbed by Talulijuk, a goddess, half-woman, half-seal, dragged underwater, towed under the ice and rammed up through the ice head first. It's written as if you believe that could or did happen.*

Houston: I certainly believe that such a thing could be. Whether anything happened in precisely that way, I don't know. There was a storm of shamanistic activity around West Baffin Island at about that time — the mid-1950s — the church really did blow away. The man [that Morgan is based on], the man without any life support, was truly seen by the people walking up on the great plain. Eleven people saw him. Now, I have written that novel from an Eskimo point of view, not saying what I thought about Morgan so much as what Shoona thought, what *they* think caused all those things to happen.

BiC: *Was there any irony in your portrayal of Morgan, an anthropologist, a southerner, a superficially weak white man, as someone who appears to have more access to the magic than the Inuit now do?*

Houston: No. Well, possibly a little bit. I think they were even. I had a little wind-up saying that the conflict hadn't yet ended and it would perhaps go on forever. It was like the Archangel Gabriel wrestling on the Plains of Heaven or something. We only witness something like that for an instant, but that conflict is one that will go on into endless time. I think Morgan was an enormously powerful person; and I felt that the most powerful shaman was old Wolf Jaw, who could hardly speak and was dying, a ruin of a man, but still he tried to go after Morgan and he apologized in the end and said he just missed.

BiC: *One last question. What's in the works now?*

Houston: I'm working on *The Fourth Eagle*, a novel about the Northwest Coast and the sea-otter trade in the early part of the 19th century. The fast ships to Canton, the beginning of the clippers. A cultural conflict between the captains, who were pretty sharp, smart dealers, and the Northwest Coast chiefs, who were quite a lot smarter than the captains were. There is a quotation from a chief there. He said, "Before the whites came, there were rivers of blood here from our fighting, from wars. But when the whites came with the trade goods, we started to trade with them and then we started to fight with *wealth*." Now, I'm interested in "fighting with wealth," and they did it in the absolute extreme — at the potlatch and so on. I'm just about finished that book. It's been a great delight to me. I live there, in the area, for study and because I hope to live there all my life. I adore it.

PHIL SURGUY

Volume 9, Number 5   A NATIONAL REVIEW OF BOOKS   May, 1980

Earle Birney recalls how CanLit boomed at UBC in the 1920s | To Sir, with yuk: a bulletin from the Grade 4 battlefield | Why P. D. James is the Jane Austen of the welfare state

BOOKSINCANADA

The craftsmanship of MORDECAI RICHLER

This copy is provided FREE by
SUBSCRIPTION PRICE: $9.95 A YEAR

1 Why did James Houston make an interesting subject for an interview?

2 You are an interviewer. Write the transcript of your interview with Phil Surguy: you wish to find out about Phil Surguy's experience in his interview with James Houston.

3 Write the blurb that will appear on the back of the jacket of James Houston's novel *Spirit Wrestler*.

Journal

A journal is a form of auto-biographical writing. The author of a journal keeps a day-by-day record of events, including impressions of those events. Often, a journal is intended for other people to read.

The Death of Evening Star

Monday, September 13, 1841

We are at sea. All ties are broken. The land is gone. I am gone. Oh, my poor mother. I shall not see her again.

Tuesday, September 14, 1841

The sea is calm these twenty-four hours.

I was everywhere today. Do this, boy — do that, boy — over here, boy — over there, boy — step lively, boy — look alive, boy. I am sore with aches and bruises. I helped Gummy for a time in the galley. Afterward, Mr. Starkweather, a boatsteerer, had me stow his lances and irons in a whaleboat. Mr. Curtis and Mr. Milton, boatsteerers, too, stowed their own harpoons. I did some errands for Mr. Franklin, the blacksmith, and Irish O'Brien, ship's carpenter. Once Mr. Hutchinson inquired after my well-being, but he walked quickly by before I could answer him. There was much activity.

Wednesday, September 15, 1841

The sea is rolling as is this ship. There has been a light rain. Everything is damp and sticky. I do not feel well. Mostly I am frightened. I was below somewhere when I became confused as to which direction I was headed. I heard some voices. I saw some figures. I was about to seek their aid — to be pointed aright — when all at once I could not. Someone in the shadows behind me clapped a huge hand over my mouth and held me fast. At that moment I saw the figures more clearly. There — on his knees — was the man I saw on that first night being dragged and beaten. Above him stood Mr. Goodspeed and the captain Mr. Hutchinson! Suddenly, Mr. Goodspeed kicked the wretched man still. He and the captain departed. Whereupon the hand dropped from my mouth and I came face to face with a large black man who quickly told me he was Ezra January and that I was to follow him. I did. We got the poor beaten man into the crew's quarters nearby where I discovered that he was known to me — a traveling peddler who came through Mystic every summer. He was known only as "Buttons" owing to his trade — he sold brass buttons. No one knew his true name or where he came from. Mr. January sent me off to my locker with a word not to speak of these events to anyone. I told no one of what I saw now or before.

Thursday, September 16, 1841

I have not eaten. I am unable to. The weather is foul. The sea heaves. I heave. There is little activity. I am more ill than I know. My end is near.

Friday, September 17, 1841

Calm the waters, dear Lord. Calm this ship, dear Lord. I am sick and finished. I pray for my salvation. Help me, please, dear Lord.

Sunday, September 19, 1841

I have been heard. The sea has improved. I am better. The ship is steady. The captain held a service today. He thanked God for our deliverance. There was no work today — it being the Sabbath. I did clean up the galley, however.

Buttons was at the service. He looked gray and distant. His face is bruised. His enemies are powerful here.

Monday, September 20, 1841

Eight days at sea. I am too far from all I love and going farther. Our heading has been due east these twenty-four hours. The wind is fair and warm. The sea is very blue. Two boats were lowered into the water this morning. Mr. Hansen and Mr. Goodspeed each took a crew of six to practice. Mr. Dixwell took his six in the afternoon. The labors have been well planned out. There are the officers who have their stations and particular duties. There are the shipkeepers — the coopers, blacksmith, carpenter, cook and me. We are expected to handle the ship while the mast hands — the rest of the crew — are hunting, killing, cutting and boiling the beasts — the great whales.

Tuesday, September 21, 1841

Our heading is still due east. We are running very smoothly. The breeze is stiff and warm. Gummy tells me that we are on the northern edge of the Gulf Stream south of the Grand Banks.

Thursday, September 23, 1841

I was too tired to make an entry last night. I am less tired now. When I am not in the galley I am with Mr. Franklin and his hot irons or with Cockeye and another cooper, Mr. Henry Clarke. Cockeye says we are going to need all these barrels for our treasure. He means whale oil.

I saw Buttons in the rigging. He is much afraid up there. He almost fell to his certain death yesterday. He caught his foot in a line and dangled in the air upside down — screaming. Some of the mast hands came to him, put a line around him, freed his foot and lowered him to the deck. Mr. Goodspeed laughed and sent him back up. Several of the men protested this. It did no good.

LEONARD EVERETT FISHER

First Trip to the Kill

This is about when my dad and I went on a first trip to get a load of the moose meat (from yesterday's kill). We started early in the morning about 7:00 a.m. I went first leading the dogs on a path through the dark, green trees. I stopped near the shoreline, my dad asked me to stop so I stopped. And he led the dogs. We didn't hitch the dogs on the shoreline. Just about in the middle of the lake we saw fox tracks. We kept going on and on.

So we got to the shore and went to a little path that led to a little stream to where he killed them. There was a hill, rocky, burned and uneven. There were little pine trees. It looked ever so nice as it was. Soon we arrived to the little stream. We hitched the dogs.

Soon Eva and Jonas arrived. My dad chopped trees down to put across. After he chopped he put them across. He said, "We are going to swim across the stream." He was teasing me. I said nothing, just smiled a little. And we went across.

Eva and I went to see the little male moose first and at last we saw the big male moose. After that,

we saw all of them. Our father told us to make our tea and lunch and we went down the hill and started a fire. First we cut burned logs and branches. Next I got a pail of water while Eva was cutting a tree to sit on. After I got a pail of water we started a fire. We talked while we worked. Then I cut a stick to hold the kettle. It was a big fire. It easily boiled. First, Eva's pot, then next our teapot. Then after we finished boiling tea we went up the hill and told them we finished boiling tea.

Then my grandpa said, "Take the heart down the hill." Then I took it down. And I put it in clean snow and cleaned it. I took the blood out. Because I don't want to eat blood for my lunch. Then my dad and grandpa came. Eva asked her dad, "What are we going to do with the heart?" He answered, "We are going to roast it."

Then he made two sticks white like a beaver does. He used his knife. Then he cut the heart in half and then he flattened it. Then he put it near the fire, on the sticks. We all drank tea, then my dad went to the small male moose. And he cut it into smaller pieces. I looked at him cutting. After he cut we went and ate our lunch. We ate roasted heart and pancake. It tasted good! First time I ate it. My dad ate our half a little bit, and I just about ate it all.

After we ate our lunch my dad made another tea and my grandfather, too, made it. After that, he drank tea. He took the moose meat to the other side of the stream. Then I took the pail, cup, tea, rolled oats and a little bit of roasted heart. Then they all took the meat, too. They said, "Come, we are starting home."

Then I went with the bag. My dad hitched the dogs to the sled. Then he was putting the meat on the sled. My grandfather, too. I went first leading the dogs. We came home about 4:30. It was dark. It's November 19, 1969. Tired bones!

SOPHIA AND SAUL WILLIAMS

1 Why are these two people keeping journals?

2 What if Buttons had also kept a journal? Write his entry for September 23, 1841.

3 Using the pattern of "First Trip to the Kill," write the journal entry for the first time that you ate an unusual food.

4 Write a free-verse poem called "The eating of the heart," based on the events in "First Trip to the Kill."

Kinetic poetry

Kinetic poetry presents the words of a poem in motion. The graphic representation must give the reader the sound, the shape, and the meaning. The print determines how the poem should be read aloud.

1 In groups, create an oral interpretation of this kinetic poem.

2 Write a kinetic poem based on another nursery rhyme. Use this parody as a pattern.

3 Find an example of kinetic poetry in an advertisement, a magazine layout, or a novel, where the graphic pattern makes a found poem.

Hark, Hark, the Dogs Do Bark

HARK, HARK,
THE DOGS DO
BARK
THE NEIGHBORS YELL,
THE BABIES CRY,
THE BUSES GRIND,
THE TELEPHONES RING, THE BONGOS BONG,
THE JET PLANES FLY, HONK,
THE CAR HORNS

THE TAXIS SCREECH,
THE RADIO'S ON, THE ROCK-
THE TEEVEE'S HIGH, AND-ROLL
THE SUBWAY ROARS POURS FROM THE RECORD STORES,
THE OLD WOMEN MUTTER
THE RATS ALONG THE GUTTER,
SQUEAK,
THE FLIES BUZZ:
Only the roaches quietly crawl.

EVE MERRIAM

Legend

The Long-haired Boy

There was a boy in our town with long hair —
I mean really long hair —
And everybody pointed at him
And laughed at him
And made fun of him.
And when he walked down the street
The people would roar
And stick their tongues out
And make funny faces
And run in and slam their door
And shout at him from the window
Until he couldn't stand it anymore.
So he sat down and cried
Till his whole body shook,
And pretty soon his hair shook too,
And it flapped
And flapped —
And he lifted —
And flew —
Straight up in the air like a helicopter.
Jenny Ricks saw him and dropped her
Knitting and screamed, "It's a flying kid!"
Lukey Hastings ran and hid
Under Old Man Merrill's car,
Miss Terance fainted, Henry Quist
Tried to shoot him down, but missed —
"I thought he was a crow," he said.
And 'round he sailed all through the day,
Smiling in the strangest way,
With the wind in his hair
And the sun in his eyes.
We saw him swoop and bank and rise.
He brushed the treetops
And skimmed the grass

On Yerbey's lawn and almost crashed
Right into Hansen's silo — but
Zoomed up in time and almost hit
The courthouse. Old Man Cooley bit
Right through his napkin when he saw
A kid fly through the diner door —
And out of the window, tipping the ladder —
Where Smokey was painting, he almost had a
Heart attack — he clung to a rafter.
The kid flew on —
Us runnin' after,
Cheering and sweating
And screaming, "Hooray!"
Mayor Lowry shouted, "Hey —
Come down here, kid. We'd like to say
How proud of you we are today.
Who ever thought our little
Town would have a hero in it?
So I'd like to proclaim this day — hey, kid!
Will you please come down for just a minute?"
But the flying kid did not come down.
He treaded air above the town,
Sort of cryin' and looking down
At all of us here on the ground.
Then up he flew, up into the clouds,
Flapping and flying so far and high,
Out past the hills and into the sky
Until a tiny speck against the sun
Was all we could see of him . . . then he was
  gone.

SHEL SILVERSTEIN

The Sky Has Fallen

One time Coyote met a turkey, and he ran and said, "Oh, the sky is falling." The turkey said, "How do you know?" "A piece of the sky has fallen on my tail. I am looking for a hole to save myself." "May I go with you?" "Come along." As they went they met a rooster, and Coyote said, "Oh, the sky is falling." The rooster said, "How do you know?" "A piece of the sky has fallen on my tail. I am looking for a hole to save myself." "May I go with you?" "Come along." As they went they met a lamb, and Coyote said, "Oh, the sky is falling." The lamb said, "How do you know?" "A piece of the sky has fallen on my tail. I am looking for a hole to save myself." "May I go with you?" "Come along." As they went they met a goose, and Coyote said, "Oh, the sky is falling." The goose said, "How do you know?" "A piece of the sky has fallen on my tail. I am looking for a hole to save myself." "May I go with you?" "Come along." At last they came to a hole and, when they were in, Coyote turned and ate the goose. When he had eaten the goose he ate the lamb. When he had eaten the lamb he ate the rooster. When he had eaten the rooster he ate the turkey. He ate them all up and these animals never came out any more.

ZUNI LEGEND

Merlin and the Snake's Egg

All night the tall young man
   Reads in his Book of Spells,
Learning the diagrams,
   The chants and stratagems
And words to serve him well
   When he's the world's magician.
But he needs the snake's egg.

The night is thick as soot,
   The dark wind's at rest,
The fire's low in the grate.
   Where he lies at Merlin's feet
The black dog stirs and moans.
   Dreams trouble his sleep.
Will they search for the snake's egg?

For the purest of magic
   Four things must be found:
Green cress from the river,
   Gold herbs from the ground,
The top twig of the high oak,
   And the snake's round, white egg.
Will they find the snake's egg?

Early, before white dawn
   Disturbs the sleeping world,
Merlin is on his way
   To the forbidden wood.
Glain, the old black dog,
   Steps where his master walked.
They go for the snake's egg.

Glain, are yours the sharp eyes
   To see where the leaf turns?
To know that small, dark hole
   Where the mouse's eye burns?
Can your ears pick up the sound
   Of the mole's breath underground?
Can you find the snake's egg?

Merlin stands at the water's edge,
   At the river's flood.
He stands in the salmon's scales,
   His blood is the salmon's blood.
He swims in the slanting stream,
   In the white foam a whiter gleam.
He has pulled the green cresses.

Merlin stands in the wide field
   Where the small creatures hide.
His long, straight limbs are lost,
   He is changed to a spider.
He crawls on crooked legs, his head
   Moves from side to side.
He has cropped the gold herbs.

Merlin stands beneath the oak.
   Feathers sprout from his arms.
His nose is an owl's hooked nose,
   His voice one of night's alarms,
His eyes are the owls' round eyes,
   Silent and soft he flies.
He has brought down the top twig.

But Glain in the troubled wood
   Steadfastly searches.
The day's last light leans in
   Under the bushes.
And there, like a little moon,
   Pale, round, and shining,
He has found the snake's egg.

LESLIE NORRIS

1 What issues are these storytellers attempting to convey? What is the basis for each of these legends?

2 Re-write the legend "The Sky Has Fallen," using human characters.

3 Write the legend of Merlin as he re-lives his youth and tells King Arthur the story of finding the snake's egg.

4 Using the details of "The Long-haired Boy," create the legend of the long-haired boy who arrived in a town, apparently from nowhere.

Letter

A Note from Miss Kelly

Dear Mrs. Peck,
Your son Robert made a rude remark to Miss Boland, our school nurse. Perhaps it was not intended to be as coarse as it sounded. Miss Boland thinks that you (his mother) should be informed of this. I quite agree.

Miss Kelly

ROBERT NEWTON PECK

Last Letter (from Norman Bethune)

Dear General Nieh:
I am fatally ill.
I am going to die.
I have some last favours
to ask of you.

Tell them I have
been happy here,
and my only regret
is that I shall not
be able to do more.

My two cots are for
you and Mrs. Nieh.
My two pairs of English
shoes also go to you.

My riding boots and trousers
I should like to
give to General Lu.

Division Commander Ho
can select what he pleases
from among my things
as a memento from me.

I would like to give
a blanket each to
Shou, my attendant,
and Chang, my cook.

A pair of Japanese shoes
should also go to Shou.

We need 250 pounds of quinine
and 300 pounds of iron compounds
each year. These are for
the malaria and anemia patients.

Never buy medicine
in such cities as
Paoting,
Tientsin and
Peiping again.
The prices there
are twice as much
as in Shanghai
and Hong Kong.

Tell them I have been
very happy. My only regret
is that I shall now
be unable to do more.

The last two years
have been the most significant,
the most meaningful years
of my life. Sometimes it
has been lonely, but I have
found my highest fulfillment
here among my beloved comrades.

I have no strength now
to write more. . . . To you
and to all my comrades,
a thousand thanks.

JOHN ROBERT COLOMBO

Vic Dardick
Box 321 High Level, Alta
Oct 26 - 72

Dear Peter.

I want to thanck you for prasing my letter and reading it on the air. I am sorry to say I did'nt hear it but my Father and several others have. I was welding in the Locall welding shop when my Father tor in there shaking my hand and congradulating me he was as happy as a kid at Christ Mass. I must admit I was surprised to say the least. I sure would like to have heard how you got around all them spelling misstakes and everrthing I think you should be congratulated on being abul to read it. I got som letters from people across Canada and they wont me to write more. Tell me Peter do you think you could batel your way threw another letter.

I won't be abule to write to you about oure wild stalion eny more. Last winter was a tuff one with lots of deep snow and steady cold wether of -30 to -55° C for 2 months

His old mair did'nt make it but this spring we saw him and his 2 year old son come out of the bush into our hayfield and we were verry happy that the old boy had an hair to his thron for he surly was a King a thrill just to watch him run with his long main and tail flying in the wind holding his head high defying enyone to catch him. His colt was a carbon copy of him and it was beutiful

Well like everry where in this world thure has to be a mean hartless person who can not stand beuty or can not see it only that this wild thing might cost him money and it might tramp down some of his presus crop so he had to shoot this noble animal and his Colt.

There are tears in my eyes as I write this not that other wild hores havent been shot in this contry but he was one of the verry last. Because he was to clever to be snared or traped he had to be shot Never again will you or I see sutch a thing of beuty a linck from the past when thowsands of sutch noble animals romed this earth wild and free.
Can you tell me why Peter Why?
Maybe I am to emotionl to think thees things out clealy But that old horse was seen hear 18 years ago. Years before most of these home steders arived. Was it the horses falt that we cleard the land and planted rich crops where he used to run free?

So sorry I have sutch a sad letter to write.

Yours truly

Vic Dardick

P.S.
I wonder if it is possible for you to send me a recording of you reading that first letter. I will gladly pay anything for it

Oct. 20, 1975

Gentlemen:
I am not a person who generally writes letters. However, in this case, I felt that I had to.

Sincerely,
David B. Carroll

Drawing by Ziegler: Copyright © The New Yorker Magazine, Inc.

1 What does the situation in each of these letters tell you about the type of letter?
2 What emotion is expressed by each of the letter writers? How does their emotion, and the problem of transcribing their thoughts into words, affect their writing style?
3 Reply to Miss Kelly as if you were Mrs. Peck. Explain the reasons for Robert's behaviour.
4 Choose a famous person and write his or her "Last Letter" as if it were a will.
5 Re-create the story of "The Last Wild Stallion" as a free-verse poem.
6 Gobbledygook is defined as "pompous, wordy, usually meaningless writing." Write a gobbledygook letter to the editor about an important issue — make sure that you don't say anything.

List

A list is a series of words selected by a writer for a particular purpose. A list can be arranged consecutively, chronologically, or randomly, but the end product must have impact.

A Checklist of Fears

Being a passenger in an airplane
Hypodermic needles
Strange dogs
Noise of vacuum cleaners
Moving to a new home
Speaking in public
Being teased
Bats
Tough-looking people
Being watched working
Dead animals
Crawling insects
Being in an elevator
Being ignored
Traveling through tunnels and traveling over
   bridges.

Jamaica Market

Honey, pepper, leaf-green limes,
Pagan fruit whose names are rhymes,
Mangoes, breadfruit, ginger-roots,
Granadillas, bamboo-shoots,
Cho-cho, ackees, tangerines,
Lemons, purple Congo-beans,
Sugar, okras, kola-nuts,
Citrons, hairy coconuts,
Fish, tobacco, native hats,
Gold bananas, woven mats,
Plantains, wild-thyme, pallid leeks,
Pigeons with their scarlet beaks,
Oranges and saffron yams,
Baskets, ruby guava jams,
Turtles, goat-skins, cinnamon,
Allspice, conch-shells, golden rum.
Black skins, babel — and the sun
That burns all colors into one.

AGNES MAXWELL-HALL

1 What is listed in each of these selections?
2 Write an inventory listing all the significant incidents in your life.
3 Write a list poem glorifying all the qualities of fast foods in North America. Base it on "Jamaica Market."
4 Invent a superstition to accompany several of the fears in the "Checklist of Fears."

Lyric poetry

A lyric poem is a songlike work, often with the theme of nature's beauty, expressing the poet's happiness and emotion.

Dream of the Black Mother

To My Mother

Black mother
Rocks her son
And in her black head
Covered with black hair
She keeps marvellous dreams.

Black mother
Rocks her son
And forgets
That the earth has dried up the maize
That yesterday the groundnuts were finished.

She dreams of marvellous worlds
Where her son would go to school
To school where men study.

Black mother
Rocks her son
And forgets
Her brothers building towns and cities
Cementing them with their blood.

She dreams of marvellous worlds
Where her son would run along the street
The street where men pass by.

Black mother
Rocks her son
And listening
To the voice from afar
Brought by the wind.

She dreams of marvellous worlds,
Marvellous worlds
Where her son will be able to live.

KALUNGANO

And my heart soars

The beauty of the trees,
the softness of the air,
the fragrance of the grass,
speaks to me.

The summit of the mountain,
the thunder of the sky,
the rhythm of the sea,
speaks to me.

The faintness of the stars,
the freshness of the morning,
the dew drop on the flower,
speaks to me.

The strength of fire,
the taste of salmon,
the trail of the sun,
And the life that never goes away,
They speak to me.

And my heart soars.

CHIEF DAN GEORGE

1 How are these poems like songs?
2 Create the song that is brought from afar by the wind to the black mother in "Dream of the Black Mother" as she rocks her son.

Melodrama

Count Dracula

WESLEY. (*As he enters.*) You buzzed twice, didn't you? I was stretched out, catching my breath after that chase across the valley.

HENNESSEY. Take over the wards, will you, Wesley? I'll be upstairs keeping watch on Miss Murray while the Doctor's out. . . . Renfield locked up tight?

WESLEY. We put him in 14-A. He'll never break out of there.

HENNESSEY. I wouldn't bet. And the key?

WESLEY. Safe. Right here. (*From jacket pocket produces key with easily identifiable red tag, holds it up.*)

HENNESSEY. (*Mounting Right stairs.*) Good. Tidy up a bit here, will you? Use that tray from the bar.

WESLEY. Righto! (*Slips key into pocket, heads for bar.*)

HENNESSEY. (*From landing, calls upstairs.*) Miss Seward, I'll take over. Wouldn't you like to go back to your own room?

SYBIL. (*Off Right upstairs.*) Oh, splendid! (HENNESSEY *exits above.*)

(WESLEY *gets bar tray, collects used glasses from end table, one from mantel, others from desk, empties ashtrays, etc. As he returns to bar with tray, his back is to the windows. Window draperies are suddenly,* violently flung back *and* COUNT DRACULA *stands there, holding drapery edges at arms' length, his cape spread wide behind him like the wings of an enormous bat. He is in his immaculate white tie and tails and wears, as well, an evil smile.* DRACULA *steps forward and the draperies fall back into place behind him.*)

DRACULA. Good evening. (WESLEY *turns, gasps, backs away fast to Left corner of bar, too frightened to yell.* DRACULA *goes to him. His tone is silken.*) I startled you, didn't I?

WESLEY. (*Whimpering in terror.*) Lord! Oh, Lord! (*As* DRACULA *approaches,* WESLEY *backs away with* DRACULA *following to Down Center. There, with a quick movement,* DRACULA *steps below him, all but blotting him from view with his cape.*)

DRACULA. Don't be alarmed. I'm Dr. Seward's neighbor — from across the valley. (*Steps away from* WESLEY, *turns front, pocketing a small unseen object.*)

WESLEY. (*Stammering.*) Then you — you must be— be Count—Count—

DRACULA. Correct.

WESLEY. S-sorry, s-sir. I was a b-b-bit startled.

DRACULA. Evidently. The good Doctor is away?

WESLEY. Yes. Yes, sir.

DRACULA. (*Relishing the word.*) How *unfortunate.* Will you ask his ubiquitous sister if she will see Count Dracula? (SOUND: *At the mention of his name,* DOGS BEGIN HOWLING *in distance.* WESLEY, *repeating* DRACULA'S *name over and over like a litany under his breath, runs up Right stairs and exits.* DRACULA *smiles, holds up the key with red tag, then slips it back into a vest pocket.* DOGS' HOWLING GROWS LOUDER. DRACULA *turns, gestures toward* WINDOW DRAPERIES *which* OPEN *at his silent command. Another gesture and* GAUZE CURTAINS OPEN *and finally* FRENCH WINDOWS OPEN OUTWARD *of their own accord. As windows open* WIND *sends gauze curtains billowing into the room. Across the valley we see Castle Carfax again and its tallest tower is dark.* DOGS' HOWLING GROWS LOUDER STILL. DRACULA *goes to window and looks out. Calls toward his castle.*) Yes, yes, I hear you. Your howling is music, a dirge for the damned! For Mina—who soon will be one of us! (HOWLING INCREASES *and* DRACULA *laughs.*) That's it! Yelp your approval for the evil I shall do this night. Yowl and whine your derision for the fools who would stop me, the little men who will try to protect her. Mina shall die—and, in death, be my bride forever in the world of the Undead! (WESLEY *races down Right steps and, without breaking stride, moves rapidly Down Right.*)

WESLEY. Miss Seward's coming, sir.

DRACULA. Of course she is coming. I willed her to come.

WESLEY. Yes, sir. Anything you say, sir! (*Runs out Down Right.*)

(DRACULA *turns to balcony again, raises one hand. Immediately the* HOWLING STOPS, *the* WIND DIES *and the billowing* CURTAINS FALL INTO PLACE *and hang motionless.* SYBIL *descends Right stairs.*)

DRACULA (*Coming downstage.*) Ah, Miss Seward! A vision, as always.

SYBIL. Good evening, Count Dracula. I'm afraid you can't see Mina tonight. She's—she's indisposed and—(*Pleased with a sudden inspiration.*) still dreadfully despondent over her friend Lucy's death, so—

DRACULA. Ah, yes. Lucy Westenra. (*Straight faced.*) We had a passing acquaintance.

SYBIL. Well, Dr. Seward said Mina was not to be disturbed.

DRACULA. Dear lady, I did not come to see Miss Murray. (*Bows over her hand, kisses it.*) I came to see you! (*Leads her to swivel chair, seats her with a lordly flourish.*) In fact, I have brought you a gift.

SYBIL. A gift? How exciting. (DRACULA *steps above her and behind swivel chair, produces small, bright gold locket on slender chain from his vest pocket, holds it out just beyond her face. SYBIL starts to put on bifocals, but vanity prevails. She squints near-sightedly at the locket.*) A gold locket? How old fashioned. I mean—how lovely!

DRACULA. It has been in my family for generations. I want you to have it. See how it shines, how it catches the firelight. (*He sways it gently before her face. Unwittingly, SYBIL becomes a spectator at a tennis match. Her eyes follow the locket from left to right, her head turns slightly from side to side as the gleaming gold swings before her. DRACULA'S voice becomes softer, intimate, almost caressing.*) Long ago, whatever goldsmith made it had you in mind. It was created to adorn your lovely throat.

SYBIL. (*Eyelids growing heavy.*) Oh, Count Dracula, I don't know how to—

DRACULA. (*Still swaying locket.*) Sh-h-h! Do not speak. You are tired. You must rest. Close your eyes and sleep. (*Whispering.*) Sleep. S-l-e-e-p. (*Her eyes close, her head droops and falls forward. DRACULA smiles malevolently, pockets the locket, spins the swivel chair so that she faces him. He cups her chin, lifts her inert head so that it lolls over the chair back. His voice no longer caresses.*) You are asleep and yet awake. Your subconscious receives and remembers every word I say. . . . But you will not remember tonight's encounter. I have not been here. You have not seen me. Do you understand?

SYBIL. (*Tonelessly.*) I understand.

DRACULA. You are now a menial, my servant, and will do whatever I demand.

SYBIL. (*Monotonously as a parrot.*) Whatever-you-demand. Whatever-you-demand. (DRACULA *spins swivel chair in a half circle so SYBIL is facing audience. Her expression is blank, her eyes unseeing.*)

DRACULA. Stand up! (SYBIL *rises.*) You will now go to the wards, release the patient Renfield and bring him here. . . . The key. (DRACULA *gives her the key. She takes a few steps Right, holding key before her with its tag dangling. Then she stops.*) Ah, yes. I read your mind. You fear you will be seen by the attendants. Forget them. They are idling in their quarters. Go! Bring Renfield to me! (SYBIL *continues on her way and exits Down Right. DRACULA laughs exultantly. A gust of* WIND *billows the curtains again and* DRACULA *goes to windows, looks up at the night sky.*) Ah, the night, the night! Would that the sun never shone, that night would last forever! (SOUND: *LOW, MOURNFUL HOWLING OF DOGS in the distance.*) That's right, my ravenous, slathering friends. You agree with me. (*Then, a gesture of dismissal.*) Enough. Begone! (SOUND: *HOWLING DIES AWAY.* DRACULA *goes swiftly up Right stairs to landing, looks up toward second floor. Then, apparently from the air, he produces the long chiffon scarf* MINA *wore at the end of Act One. Descending steps, he kisses it, fondles it, tucks it into inner pocket. Once more he causes a flaming cigarette to appear from nowhere, blows out the flame and is smoking lazily when* SYBIL *enters Down Right leading* RENFIELD *by the hand.*) Well done. You will make an excellent servant.

RENFIELD. Master, she —

DRACULA. Silence! She must know nothing. (*Approaches* SYBIL.) When this hypnotic state has passed, you will recall nothing that has transpired.

SYBIL. (*An automaton.*) Nothing that has transpired.

DRACULA. But when again I need you, your mind, your will are powerless to resist me. Repeat that.

SYBIL. My mind, my will are powerless to resist you. (DRACULA *laughs, joined by* RENFIELD *who is silenced by an imperious gesture.*)

DRACULA. (*To* SYBIL.) Go to your room. (*She obediently starts to Right staircase.*) No! That will not do. (*She stops.*) Hennessey is upstairs. He must not see you hypnotized. Let me consider. (*In thought, and not seeming to notice, he puts burning cigarette into his loosely closed hand as though extinguishing it. When he opens the hand, the cigarette has vanished.*) Go instead to your music room. (SYBIL *turns, starts Left.*) Devote your addled brain to the scores of Bach, Purcell, Handel. Confound your minuscule intelligence with their hemi-demi-semi-quavers. (SYBIL *mounts Left stairs at sleepwalker's pace and exits.* DRACULA *turns sharply to* RENFIELD *who crumples to his knees.*) Now, you! I have work for you.

TED TILLER

1 What do the dialogue, setting, and stage directions in this selection tell you about melodrama?

2 As a class, plot the action of the rest of this play to its melodramatic climax.

3 Choose one incident in the plot that you have devised and write the setting, stage directions, and dialogue for it.

81

Memoir

The author of a memoir is concerned with re-creating the times that he or she has lived through. The author is similar to a reporter, commenting on people and events, but the author of a memoir adds his or her emotional responses to the story.

The Chip Wagon

When the whistle on the roof of the chip wagon blew, it was like a Pied Piper calling us kids — and just as irresistible.

Even though in winter the chip wagons changed their wheels for sleigh runners, we still called them "chip wagons," never chip sleighs. And although we ate from them the year round, their marvelous french-fried potatoes and steamed hot dogs never tasted so good as in winter. The chip wagons usually stopped after school hours at municipal skating rinks, and on Saturdays and Sundays at Fletchers Field on Mount Royal where skiers and tobogganers were out in numbers. No matter what ingredients and love our mothers used, their french-fried potatoes never tasted as good as the chipman's. You could smell the wonderful aroma even before you got close to the wagon. The chips were served in paper cones, always greasy and always wonderfully warm to the touch for cold, young hands. There was vinegar for the chips and mustard and cabbage for the hot dogs. If you had an extra dime, a rare thing, you could also get hot buttered popcorn and even hotter roasted peanuts in the shell. Many chip wagons, especially in Montreal's north end, were operated by people of Ukrainian origin.

While the whistle on the roof blew and the windows fogged up, the chipman shook the basket of his deep fryer, turned valves, pumped fuel, and dispensed happiness.

CARLO ITALIANO

"The Chip Wagon" reprinted from *The Sleighs of My Childhood/Les traîneaux de mon enfance* © 1974 Carlo Italiano, published by Tundra Books of Montreal.

"Lumberjack's Breakfast" reprinted from *Lumberjack* © 1974 William Kurelek, published by Tundra Books of Montreal.

Lumberjack's Breakfast

The lumberjack's day began when a cookee sounded the camp gong. This consisted of using a bar of iron to hit a piece of railway track that had been suspended on a wire near the cook shack door. Its message was clear: "Get up, boys! Wash up!" — or at least "Get dressed!" Twenty minutes later the second gong said, "Breakfast's on and the cookhouse door is open."

All meals were hefty. Hard work and fresh air gave us voracious appetites which we were so busy satisfying that we hardly talked. I found myself eating three times as much as I had back home.

At breakfast the table was heaped with plates of flapjacks, mountains of them, big bowls of porridge and tin dishes of fried baloney, bacon, potatoes, beans and stacks of camp-baked bread. Enamelware jugs held tea, coffee and milk; the milk came from cans. I missed the natural milk I was used to.

Each cookee was assigned a table and he hung around eyeing the plates in case any needed a refill. We were charged only $1.25 a day then for room and board, but if you weren't working for some reason, even that could seem quite expensive. If you slept late, or didn't get back from work on time, you went hungry until the next meal.

WILLIAM KURELEK

1 Why are these selections called "memoir" rather than "autobiography"?

2 Write a memoir that explains your remembrance of a fair or concert. Discuss the impact of the event on all of your senses.

3 Imagine that you are writing your memoir, looking back at your youth. Describe a weekend breakfast at your home.

4 It is the year 2025. Write an editorial on "The Good Old Days."

Monologue

A monologue is a speech given by one actor. It may be long or short, serious or humorous, and on any subject.

"Of course, it wasn't easy . . ."

"Of course, it wasn't easy, and there were plenty of times when I didn't know what to do, but, God bless 'em, all the kids had gumption. Homer is a full partner in a prestigious law firm now. Daphne is a psychiatrist. Ollie is the comptroller of an enormous conglomerate. Irma's second novel has just gone into its seventeenth printing. Osgood is a top-echelon TV-network executive. Penelope is a professor of oceanography at a large university. Louis is concertmaster of a world-famous symphony orchestra. Miriam owns a chain of highly successful boutiques. Elsie ran for the legislature and won by a landslide. Mortimer is the chief geologist for a giant oil company. Gertrude is vice-president of a big advertising agency. Herman is a plastic surgeon with a huge practice. And little Jerome, the baby of the lot, has his very own Ph.D. and heads an important research group that analyzes the media, bless his heart."

Drawing by Wm. Miller: Copyright © The New Yorker Magazine, Inc.

More Socks

MAN. I go to the laundromat to do a wash. Included in the wash are 8 pairs of socks. Out of the wash comes 6 pairs of socks plus 1 gray sock and 1 blue sock. A week later I go to the laundromat to do a wash. Included in the wash are 6 pairs of socks. Out of the wash comes 4 pairs of socks plus 1 black sock and 1 green sock. A week later I go to the laundromat to do a wash. Included in the wash are 4 pairs of socks. Out of the wash come 2 pairs of socks. The other socks never show up. The next day I go to the laundromat. As an experiment I put in nothing but my last 2 pairs of socks. Out of the wash comes a body stocking. (*He opens bundle and takes out note.*) In the body stocking I find a note. The note says: "Quit trifling with the laws of nature and bring the machine more socks."

JULES FEIFFER

A Loss of Roses

Lila — 30s — FEMALE — SERIOUS *A small-time waitress remembers a moment from her childhood.*

I remember my first day of school. Mother took me by the hand and *I* carried a bouquet of roses, too. Mama had let me pick the loveliest roses I could find in the garden, and the teacher thanked me for them. Then Mama left me and I felt kinda scared, 'cause I'd never been any place before without her; but she told me Teacher would be Mama to me at school, and would treat me just as nice as she did. So I took my seat with all the other kids, their faces so strange and new to me. And I started talking with a little boy across the aisle. I din know it was against the rules. But teacher came back and slapped me, so hard that I cried, and I ran to the door 'cause I wanted to run home to Mama quick as I could. But Teacher grabbed me by the hand and pulled me back to my seat. She said I was too big a girl to be running home to Mama and I had to learn to take my punishment when I broke the rules. But I still cried. I told Teacher I wanted back my roses. But she wouldn't give them to me. She shook her finger and said, when I gave away lovely presents, I couldn't expect to get them back . . . I guess I never learned that lesson very well. There's so many things I still want back.

WILLIAM INGE

1 Who is listening to each of these speeches?

2 From the clues in "More Socks," write a character sketch of the husband.

3 Pick another nursery rhyme and create a monologue for its main character, using the pattern of "Of course, it wasn't easy."

4 Write a monologue, based on "A Loss of Roses," from your remembrances of school.

5 Write another monologue, similar to "Strike," given by this character as she talks to a person from the past, such as Christopher Columbus or Laura Secord.

Mystery

There are many types of mystery stories: stories about secret crimes, tales of suspense and espionage, detective stories, and stories of people pursued by some unknown but frightening menace.

Mushrooms

Mushrooms grew
Overnight
        like they always did
Only this time
        there was
    nobody
    to
      pick them

MIKE EVANS

The Small Room

"I found myself in a small room. Soundlessly the doors slid shut after me and a sequential series of numbers on the wall began to light up - one after another. Some sort of countdown, I figured, or perhaps a trick. I became aware of a faint whirring sound and got the weird feeling I was being taken for a ride. Yet I was standing still! A fist tightened inside my stomach and I felt sick. My ears began to pop like cheap gum. Pop! Pop pop pop! This case was beginning to take on bizarre proportions, all right."

Drawing by Ziegler: Copyright © The New Yorker Magazine, Inc.

Knock

The last man on Earth sat alone in a room.

There was a knock at the door . . .

1 How would you classify these mystery stories?

2 You are the detective in "The Small Room." You find yourself in another "bizarre" place. Write the monologue.

3 Suppose that "Mushrooms" is the climax of a short mystery story. Tell the whole story.

Myth

Pandora's Box

If they had only said,
"Pandora,
go ahead
and open it right away;
you may find something useful inside:

a combination sunshade
and umbrella for a rainy day,

or something instructive,
like the tape of a lecture on
how to improve the brain;

or there well may be
some moderating capsule
to help reduce the extremes
of both pleasure and pain;

or consider! some magic crystal ball
wherein the future could be made
entirely known
and to you alone" —

in that case,
she might never have opened the box at all.

EVE MERRIAM

The Invisible Men

There is a tribe of invisible men
who move around us like shadows — have you
    felt them?
They have bodies like ours and live just like us,
using the same kind of weapons and tools.
You can see their tracks in the snow sometimes
and even their igloos
but never the invisible men themselves.
They cannot be seen except when they die
for then they become visible.
It once happened that a human woman
married one of the invisible men.
He was a good husband in every way:
He went out hunting and brought her food,
and they could talk together like any other
    couple.
But the wife could not bear the thought
that she did not know what the man she married
    looked like.
One day when they were both at home
she was so overcome with curiosity to see him
that she stabbed with a knife where she knew he
    was sitting.
And her desire was fulfilled:
Before her eyes a handsome young man fell to
    the floor.
But he was cold and dead, and too late
she realized what she had done,
and sobbed her heart out.
When the invisible men heard about this murder
they came out of their igloos to take revenge.
Their bows were seen moving through the air
and the bow strings stretching as they aimed
    their arrows.
The humans stood there helplessly
for they had no idea what to do or how to fight
because they could not see their assailants.
But the invisible men had a code of honor
that forbade them to attack opponents
who could not defend themselves,
so they did not let their arrows fly,
and nothing happened; there was no battle after
    all
and everyone went back to their ordinary lives.

NETSILIK ESKIMO

It Is So

Drawing by Booth: Copyright © The New Yorker Magazine, Inc.

The Sick Moon Ceremony

When the moon comes up in the daytime
Pale and thin
The Sick Moon ceremony is held.

The women cease gathering milkweed for twine,
Cease basket-making, and weaving.

The men put away their long willow bows,
Their quivers and arrows,
Put an end to their hunting.

And they all go down, the whole of the village,
To the stream.

They bathe, and they sport in the water,
Run foot races, joke, and tell tales.

They laugh, and the women sing
Songs to make the moon glad.

Each has her own song and she sings it,
They cure the sick moon with their fun and their
    songs.

DIEGUENO

1 What natural mysteries do each of these myths explain?

2 Using "The Sick Moon Ceremony" as a pattern, describe the myth ceremony that takes place at the eclipse of the sun.

3 Using the structure of "The Invisible Men," write a myth called "The Mask." Explore the issue that we should not attempt to remove all the masks in our lives.

4 "Pandora's Box" is based on the Greek myth in which Pandora let loose all the ills of the world by opening a forbidden box. Present several arguments to persuade Pandora not to open the box.

5 You are an anthropologist. Explain the origin of the ancient tribal myth presented in "It Is So!"

Narrative poetry

> A narrative poem tells a story. The story can be presented from the viewpoint of a character in the poem or of a narrator.

The Dairy Queen

I was sitting there eating a strawberry sundae
and looking at a sign on the door reading Coca-
    Cola PUSH
and thinking I'd like to get one of those next
    time
and I was quietly observing two young girls
with blue paint precociously under their eyes
who were giggling at this moderately old woman
who had just come into the place raving like a
merry old prophet: *There's going to be*
a heck of a storm, it's really going to rain,
there's going to be thunder and lightning
and just then it started.
She was talking to no one in particular
but she had tapped into a supply of strange
    energy,
a raging river not available to most of us
and it was bursting its dams.
If I may be permitted a motoring metaphor
she had her lights on high beam
and I was becoming angry because the two
    young girls
were giggling, acting superior and sophisticated.
The woman had a large leather bag and pulled
    out
a jar of Cheeze Whiz and a package of biscuits
then asked the guy behind the counter for a
    knife.
He gave her one and she sat down and began
    spreading
the cheese onto the biscuits and eating them.
She ate about four, and I sat there wondering
about her origins, her destiny
and I had the impression she was a highly
    intelligent woman
who was afire with life, perhaps even a poet,
perhaps a poetry-writing member of the
    Canadian

Authors Association or the League of Canadian
    Poets
and I said a small prayer that I would never
have to read her poems, knowing they wouldn't
    be
half as interesting as she.

So, there was thunder and lightning booming
through the skies above the Dairy Queen, the
    rain
was coming down, a veritable torrent of spring,
and the woman put down her knife, and noticed
    it
first, as poets tend to do, she beat me to it,
she was the first to notice that with all that rain
coming down the sun was still shining
and the whole earth was radiant with
    goldenness.
Look at that, everyone, she called out.
The sun is actually shining! It's a sun-shower!
And I just kept on being as dull and dumb
as the rest of the slobs in the Dairy Queen
who were trying to pretend she wasn't there.

Is it just me getting grouchier as I get older
or is the world really getting dumber and
    dumber
as it gets older, it seems that every day
there seem to be more and more people
    wandering around
in a lifeless daze, dead, cold, hollow,
with all their lights out.
That woman, it was easy to see she was really
enjoying her cheese biscuits, not to mention
every other aspect of the moment as it
blossomed in her face
but those silly teenage girls with the blue
eye shadow under their eyes instead of on the
    lids,
they were eating their ice cream cones
as if their tongues were frozen solid
instead of warm and sensitive
and by the looks on their faces
or rather the non-looks
it was impossible to tell if they
were enjoying them or not

and I'm sure they weren't.

DAVID McFADDEN

Home Burial

He saw her from the bottom of the stairs
Before she saw him. She was starting down,
Looking back over her shoulder at some fear.
She took a doubtful step and then undid it
To raise herself and look again. He spoke
Advancing toward her: "What is it you see
From up there always? — for I want to know."
She turned and sank upon her skirts at that,
And her face changed from terrified to dull.
He said to gain time: "What is it you see?"
Mounting until she cowered under him.
"I will find out now — you must tell me, dear."
She, in her place, refused him any help,
With the least stiffening of her neck and silence.
She let him look, sure that he wouldn't see,
Blind creature; and awhile he didn't see.
But at last he murmured, "Oh," and again,
    "Oh."

"What is it — what?" she said.

                        "Just that I see."

"You don't," she challenged. "Tell me what it
    is."

"The wonder is I didn't see at once.
I never noticed it from here before.
I must be wonted to it — that's the reason.
The little graveyard where my people are!
So small the window frames the whole of it.
Not so much larger than a bedroom, is it?
There are three stones of slate and one of marble,
Broad-shouldered little slabs there in the sunlight
On the sidehill. We haven't to mind *those*.
But I understand: it is not the stones,
But the child's mound —"

                        "Don't, don't, don't,
    don't," she cried.

She withdrew, shrinking from beneath his arm
That rested on the banister, and slid downstairs;
And turned on him with such a daunting look,
He said twice over before he knew himself:
"Can't a man speak of his own child he's lost?"

"Not you! — Oh, where's my hat? Oh, I don't
    need it!
I must get out of here. I must get air. —
I don't know rightly whether any man can."

"Amy! Don't go to someone else this time.
Listen to me. I won't come down the stairs."
He sat and fixed his chin between his fists.

"There's something I should like to ask you,
    dear."

"You don't know how to ask it."

                        "Help me, then."

Her fingers moved the latch for all reply.

"My words are nearly always an offense.
I don't know how to speak of anything
So as to please you. But I might be taught,
I should suppose. I can't say I see how.
A man must partly give up being a man
With womenfolk. We could have some
    arrangement
By which I'd bind myself to keep hands off
Anything special you're a-mind to name.
Though I don't like such things 'twixt those that
    love.
Two that don't love can't live together without
    them.
But two that do can't live together with them."
She moved the latch a little. "Don't — don't go.
Don't carry it to someone else this time.
Tell me about it if it's something human.
Let me into your grief. I'm not so much
Unlike other folks as your standing there
Apart would make me out. Give me my chance.
I do think, though, you overdo it a little.
What was it brought you up to think it the thing
To take your mother-loss of a first child
So inconsolably — in the face of love.
You'd think his memory might be satisfied —"

"There you go sneering now!"

                        "I'm not, I'm not!
You make me angry. I'll come down to you.
God, what a woman! And it's come to this,
A man can't speak of his own child that's dead."

"You can't because you don't know how to
    speak.
If you had any feelings, you that dug
With your own hand — how could you? — his
    little grave;
I saw you from that very window there,
Making the gravel leap and leap in air,
Leap up, like that, like that, and land so lightly
And roll back down the mound beside the hole.
I thought, Who is that man? I didn't know you.
And I crept down the stairs and up the stairs
To look again, and still your spade kept lifting.
Then you came in. I heard your rumbling voice
Out in the kitchen, and I don't know why,
But I went near to see with my own eyes.

You could sit there with the stains on your shoes
Of the fresh earth from your own baby's grave
And talk about your everyday concerns.
You had stood the spade up against the wall
Outside there in the entry, for I saw it."

"I shall laugh the worst laugh I ever laughed.
I'm cursed. God, if I don't believe I'm cursed."

"I can repeat the very words you were saying:
'Three foggy mornings and one rainy day
Will rot the best birch fence a man can build.'
Think of it, talk like that at such a time!
What had how long it takes a birch to rot
To do with what was in the darkened parlor?
You *couldn't* care! The nearest friends can go
With anyone to death, comes so far short
They might as well not try to go at all.
No, from the time when one is sick to death,
One is alone, and he dies more alone.
Friends make pretense of following to the grave,
But before one is in it, their minds are turned
And making the best of their way back to life
And living people, and things they understand.
But the world's evil. I won't have grief so
If I can change it. Oh, I won't, I won't!"

"There, you have said it all and you feel better.
You won't go now. You're crying. Close the
    door.
The heart's gone out of it: why keep it up?
Amy! There's someone coming down the road!"

"*You* — oh, you think the talk is all. I must go —
Somewhere out of this house. How can I make
    you —"

"If — you — do!" She was opening the door
    wider.
"Where do you mean to go? First tell me that.
I'll follow and bring you back by force. I *will*! —"

ROBERT FROST

1 Who are the narrators in these poems?

2 You are the woman with the Cheez Whiz in "The
   Dairy Queen." Write your version of this scene
   as a narrative poem.

3 Imagine the poem "Home Burial" as a play. Starting with the last line of the poem, write the next
   scene, continuing the action.

Novel

A novel is an extended story. The length allows the author to develop characters, situations, and events so that the reader may become deeply involved in the relationships and events.

Burgers, Burgers, Burgers

Kenny was mopping the back sink and wearing a beige garbage bag. He had punched a hole at the top and two at the sides for his arms.

"You splashed too much water around here. And turn down the radio," said Greg as he moved closer. He tiptoed over the puddles. "Get a mop, I don't want anyone to trip."

"Sorry," said Kenny. They stood over the three sinks. The first two were filled with frothy soap suds with submerged stainless steel appliances elbowing out. Thick brown curds of grease floated randomly in the water. The third sink was filled with a Stera Sheen solution where the washed equipment was sterilized.

"You seem to be doing all right. Try and be finished by twelve-thirty."

"I'll try."

"I tell you, Kenny, I thought you were going to punch out after the first fifteen minutes of working on the floor," Greg chuckled.

"Oh yeah," said Kenny getting the mop.

"But I think you're doing just fine."

Kenny smiled. He liked fitting in. He mopped up the puddles urgently to prove his worth to Greg.

Still, something bothered him. "Hey, Greg, I got a question."

"Ask away," said Greg with a friendly tilt of his head.

"Is it really a three-month wait for a raise?"

"Nice question," said Greg. His tone assumed that Kenny was an equal. "Yes, that's how it works around here. The first three months are what we call your probationary period, after which you are eligible for a raise." Greg shrugged his shoulders. "Listen man, I just get a dollar and a half more than you." His thumb pointed to his chest. "Even though I am responsible for everything that happens after Mel leaves."

Greg looked flustered. "It's a cheap company. They offered me a straight salary that sounded really good. Little did I know that I would end up working fifty hours a week." He scratched his back thoughtfully.

"I should have known, too. I had been with them long enough," Greg continued. "I was going to State University and I needed money. So I got a job at a Benny Burger nearby." Greg laughed to himself. "And that's when they paid only a dollar ninety-five an hour." He folded his arms over his chest. "I liked it there and I worked hard and became a crew coordinator in a year. They offered me a managership. But the catch was I couldn't be a manager and go to school at the same time."

"Who said that?"

"They said that. All that money sounded so great." Greg yawned and his arms stretched, exposing his Benny Burger clip hanging limp and tired on his tie.

"All that money," Kenny repeated, savoring the thought.

Greg laughed and slapped Kenny's back. "Good boy, now finish the back sink."

"Sure thing."

JAMES TRIVERS

1 This selection is an excerpt from a novel. Kenny, the main character, has accepted a job in the Benny Burger Restaurant. What issues do you think the author will deal with in the rest of the novel?

2 Chapter One of this novel describes Kenny's first day on the job. Write the scene in which he applies for the job.

3 Write the blurb for the jacket of this novel, using the following facts: Kenny needs to earn money; he wants to buy clothes; he wants to meet girls; he hates the routine of work. He also has a dream and decides to rob the restaurant.

Obituary

An obituary is a notice of someone's death. In the obituary, the writer attempts to sum up the person's achievement and personality. Often, the obituary includes a brief biography of the dead person.

John Lennon

NEW YORK (Reuter) — John Lennon, who was shot and killed at his New York home Monday night, was born in Liverpool on Oct. 9, 1940. He knew tragedy and unhappiness at an early age, which later would have a profound effect on his music.

His father, Alfred Lennon, deserted the family when John was 3. His mother Julia, who later re-married, was killed in an automobile accident when he was 13.

When his father came out of hiding in 1964, John did not wish to renew the association.

Lennon's mother was his earliest musical influence. She played the piano and taught her son the basic banjo chords when he bought his first guitar.

Before his mother's death, Lennon lived with an aunt, Mary Smith, whom he called Aunt Mimi. She encouraged him to develop a leaning toward art.

But his over-riding enthusiasm was for pop music. In 1956 he met Paul McCartney and the pair dedicated themselves to developing their musical techniques.

In 1959, the Beatles, as the group was now calling itself, took a tramp steamer to Hamburg, West Germany.

They were a quintet at that time with drummer Pete Best and guitarist Stuart Sutcliffe. Tragically, Sutcliffe died of a brain tumor in Germany and thereafter the group remained a four-piece outfit. Best was later replaced by Ringo Starr.

On their return to Liverpool, after some success in Hamburg, they were booked in a cellar club, The Cavern. It was there that Brian Epstein came to see them.

Epstein became their manager and immediately set about getting rid of the leather jackets and greasy hairstyles they had been sporting. The hair remained long, but tidy. The jackets were now smart suits. Epstein eventually won them a recording contract, and Beatlemania began.

By November, 1963, they were appearing at a Royal Command variety performance in London attended by Princess Margaret and the Queen Mother, who visited them backstage.

Lennon and McCartney began to produce their own songs. It was one of these, I Want to Hold Your Hand, that brought them fame in the United States. The record sold four million copies, and launched them on a triumphant tour of America which included appeareances on the Ed Sullivan television show.

In February, 1964, a leading British bank declared the Beatles a national asset, saying export of their records had made a major contribution to the country's balance of payments.

The following year, recognition of this was given when Queen Elizabeth, on the recommendation of the then Labor government, named them members of the Order of the British Empire (OBE).

Lennon did not devote himself exclusively to music. He started writing at the age of 14 and had two best-selling books to his credit. Art, too, absorbed him greatly.

He met his first wife Cynthia, "over a pot of paint," while both were attending the Liverpool College of Art. They had a son — John Julian, born in 1963 — but their marriage ended in November, 1968, when Cynthia sued John for divorce, naming Yoko Ono as the other woman.

A month before the case was heard, it was announced that Miss Ono was expecting John's baby. He declared then, "Babies make the world happier and that's our scene."

In the early seventies, Lennon waged a three-year battle with the United States Immigration and Naturalization Service over his application for permanent resident status in the U.S. He was technically ineligible because of a 1968 conviction in Britain for possession of marijuana.

In October, 1975, U.S. immigration officials shelved the case on "humanitarian grounds."

Following the death of Epstein in August, 1967, Lennon brought in American businessman Allen

Klein to run the affairs of Apple, the group's own recording company. This move was opposed by Paul McCartney, who wanted his father-in-law, an American lawyer, to run their affairs.

McCartney, however, refused to cooperate with Klein, and eventually brought about a final rift among the Beatles by seeking a court order winding up the group's affairs.

REUTERS

1 Why did John Lennon deserve such a prominent obituary?

2 Newspapers frequently prepare obituaries for important people before they die. Research the life of a celebrity and write his or her obituary.

3 You have been missing and thought dead. On the day of your "funeral," you arrive home and read your obituary in the newspaper. Write that obituary.

Ode

An ode is a lyric poem that is written in honour of a person or object. It is written in a dignified and sincere manner.

Ode

So solemn and quiet they stand
Shaking in the wind
Bracing against the winter months
Year after year letting the days go by
Standing there not dying
Bearing leaves and letting them fall
    into the quiet autumn months.
They slumber in the quiet summer days
    only to awaken angry on the restless winter
    nights
They shake with anger when the night winds
    blow
Sharing secrets of the passing years
And living longer than I.

ISHITA MUKERJI

Salutation

O Generation of the thoroughly smug
    and thoroughly uncomfortable,
I have seen fishermen picnicking in the sun,
I have seen them with untidy families,
I have seen their smiles full of teeth
    and heard ungainly laughter.
And I am happier than you are,
And they were happier than I am;
And the fish swim in the lake
    and do not even own clothing.

EZRA POUND

1 Who or what is being honoured in each of these poems?

2 Choose another aspect of nature and write a poem similar to "Ode," describing and honouring that aspect.

3 The poem "Salutation" is critical of society. Choose an aspect of society that displeases you, and write a similar ode, examining and commenting on it.

An order commands someone to do something. The order is given by a person in authority, who has the power to demand obedience.

Warrant to Apprehend

Canada,
Province of Manitoba,
County of Selkirk.
To all or any of the Constables or other Peace Officers in the County of Selkirk.

Whereas Louis Riel and Ambrose Lepine and others have, this day, been charged upon oath before the undersigned, one of Her Majesty's Justices of the Peace in and for the said County of Selkirk, for that they, the said Louis Riel, Ambrose Lepine, and others unknown, did, on or about the fourth day of March, in the year of Our Lord 1870, feloniously kill and murder one Thomas Scott, at the said County of Selkirk.

These are, therefore to command you in Her Majesty's name forthwith to apprehend the said Louis Riel, Ambrose Lepine, and others, and to bring them before me or some other of Her Majesty's Justices of the Peace, in and for the said County of Selkirk, to answer unto the said charge, and to be further dealt with according to law.

Given under my hand and Seal, this 15th day of September in the year of Our Lord one thousand eight hundred and seventy-three, at the Town of Winnipeg, in the County of Selkirk, aforesaid.

John H. O'Donnell, J.P.

Orders

Muffle the wind;
Silence the clock;
Muzzle the mice;
Curb the small talk;
Cure the hinge-squeak;
Banish the thunder.
Let me sit silent,
Let me wonder.

A. M. KLEIN

1 Why have the orders in these selections been issued?

2 Write a warrant to apprehend the nuisances who destroy the environment.

3 Using the pattern of "Orders," write a poem that sets out to rid the world of visual ugliness.

Parable

> A parable is a short, simple story that illustrates a moral or that teaches a lesson.

The Parable of the Prodigal Son

And he said, A certain man had two sons:
And the younger of them said to *his* father, Father, give me the portion of goods that falleth to *me*.
And he divided unto them *his* living.
And not many days after the younger son gathered all together, and took his journey into a far country, and there wasted his substance with riotous living.
And when he had spent all, there arose a mighty famine in that land; and he began to be in want.
And he went and joined himself to a citizen of that country; and he sent him into his fields to feed swine.
And he would fain have filled his belly with the husks that the swine did eat: and no man gave unto him.
And when he came to himself, he said, How many hired servants of my father's have bread enough and to spare, and I perish with hunger!
I will arise and go to my father, and will say unto him, Father, I have sinned against heaven, and before thee,
And am no more worthy to be called thy son: make me as one of thy hired servants.
And he arose, and came to his father. But when he was yet a great way off, his father saw him, and had compassion, and ran, and fell on his neck, and kissed him.
And the son said unto him, Father, I have sinned against heaven, and in thy sight, and am no more worthy to be called thy son.
But the father said to his servants, Bring forth the best robe, and put *it* on him; and put a ring on his hand, and shoes on *his* feet:
And bring hither the fatted calf, and kill *it*; and let us eat, and be merry:
For this my son was dead, and is alive again; he was lost, and is found. And they began to be merry.
Now his elder son was in the field: and as he came and drew nigh to the house, he heard music and dancing.
And he called one of the servants, and asked what these things meant.
And he said unto him, Thy brother is come; and thy father hath killed the fatted calf, because he hath received him safe and sound.
And he was angry, and would not go in: therefore came his father out, and entreated him.
And he answering said to *his* father, Lo, these many years do I serve thee, neither transgressed I at any time thy commandment; and yet thou never gavest me a kid, that I might make merry with my friends:
But as soon as this thy son was come, which hath devoured thy living with harlots, thou hast killed for him the fatted calf.
And he said unto him, Son, thou art ever with me, and all that I have is thine.
It was meet that we should make merry, and be glad: for this thy brother was dead, and is alive again; and was lost, and is found.

ST. LUKE, HOLY BIBLE

The Man and the Angel of Death

A man was carrying a heavy load of wood on his shoulders. When he grew weary he let the bundle down and cried bitterly, "O, Death, come and take me!"

Immediately, the Angel of Death appeared and asked, "Why do you call me?"

Frightened, the man answered, "Please help me place the load back on my shoulders."

MORAL

Even though life has its griefs man prefers a life of wretchedness to death.

TRADITIONAL

Elephants are Different to Different People

Wilson and Pilcer and Snack stood before the zoo elephant.
Wilson said, 'What is its name? Is it from Asia or Africa? Who feeds it? Is it a he or a she? How old is it? Do they have twins? How much does it cost to feed? How much does it weigh? If it dies, how much will another one cost? If it

dies, what will they use the bones, the fat, and the hide for? What use is it besides to look at?'

Pilcer didn't have any questions; he was murmuring to himself, 'It's a house by itself, walls and windows, the ears come from tall cornfields, by God; the architect of those legs was a workman, by God; he stands like a bridge out across deep water; the face is sad and the eyes are kind; I know elephants are good to babies.'

Snack looked up and down and at last said to himself, 'He's a tough son-of-a-gun outside and I'll bet he's got a strong heart, I'll bet he's strong as a copper-riveted boiler inside.'

They didn't put up any arguments.
They didn't throw anything in each other's faces.
Three men saw the elephant three ways

And let it go at that.
They didn't spoil a sunny Sunday afternoon;
'Sunday comes only once a week,' they told each
  other.

CARL SANDBURG

1 What is the lesson that each of these parables teaches?

2 Re-tell ''The Parable of the Prodigal Son'' in a contemporary setting.

3 Write a sermon using ''Elephants are Different to Different People'' as the text.

4 Re-tell the parable ''The Man and the Angel of Death'' as a short story.

Parallel poetry

A parallel poem is a series of comparisons. The poem has one theme, and each of the lines describes a new aspect of the subject.

Snow is . . .

snow is english
snow is international
snow is secret
snow is small
snow is literary
snow is translatable
snow is everywhere
snow is ridiculous
snow is difficult
snow is modern
snow is hindering
snow is senseless
snow is musical
snow is gorgeous
snow is sedimentary
snow is meaningless
snow is elemental
snow is fantastic
snow is curved
snow is unauthorized

snow is disgusting
snow is ignorant
snow is irresistible
snow is rare
snow is exhausting
snow is civil
snow is smooth
snow is amusing
snow is epidemic
snow is hereditary
snow is risky
snow is analyzable
snow is satisfactory
snow is catholic
snow is tasteless
snow is elegant
snow is absolute
snow is experimental
snow is neurotic
snow is instructive

snow is selfish
snow is unique
snow is prepared
snow is expensive
snow is alphabetical
snow is unsocial
snow is sexless
snow is political
snow is provisional
snow is predominant
snow is reasonable
snow is violet
snow is distracting
snow is looking
snow is utopian
snow is evangelic
snow is inevitable
snow is cheap
snow is comprehensible
snow is delicious
snow is relative
snow is norwegian
snow is military
snow is comfortable
snow is light
snow is salutary
snow is harmful
snow is cold
snow is offensive
snow is brute
snow is scientific

snow is irregular
snow is indefensible
snow is independent
snow is annoying
snow is sad
snow is enormous
snow is pale
snow is barefooted
snow is corrupt
snow is cordial
snow is converse
snow is libidinous
snow is permitted
snow is sublime
snow is tawdry
snow is imaginable
snow is abstinent
snow is exact
snow is etymological
snow is fragmentary
snow is honorable
snow is immortal
snow is ancient
snow is illustrative
snow is aristotelian
snow is outside
snow is abstract
snow is divine
snow is white
snow is contradictory

EUGEN GOMRINGER

1 This selection is an expanded definition of snow. Is it a poem?

2 Using the thesaurus, write a parallel poem that defines one of the following subjects: water, fire, earth, air, wind, rain.

3 Write a character study of yourself in the form of a parallel poem. Start with "I am . . ."

Parody

A parody is an imitation of another piece of writing. Its purpose is to poke fun at or criticize the original.

1 What is being parodied in these selections?

2 Continue the parody of the dialogue in this scene from "Flight 1313."

3 Imagine the parody "Blazing Blades" as a film. Write a summary of the climax of the film.

Flight 1313

Blazing Blades

Philosophy

A philosopher analyzes a subject in order to gain new insights into it.

Thirteen Ways of Looking at a Blackbird

I Among twenty snowy mountains,
The only moving thing
Was the eye of the blackbird.

II I was of three minds,
Like a tree
In which there are three blackbirds.

III The blackbird whirled in the autumn winds.
It was a small part of the pantomime.

IV A man and a woman
Are one.
A man and a woman and a blackbird
Are one.

V   I do not know which to prefer,
The beauty of inflections
Or the beauty of innuendoes,
The blackbird whistling
Or just after.

VI   Icicles filled the long window
With barbaric glass.
The shadow of the blackbird
Crossed it, to and fro.
The mood
Traced in the shadow
An indecipherable cause.

VII   O thin men of Haddam,
Why do you imagine golden birds?
Do you not see how the blackbird
Walks around the feet
Of the women about you?

VIII   I know noble accents
And lucid, inescapable rhythms;
But I know, too,
That the blackbird is involved
In what we know.

IX   When the blackbird flew out of sight,
It marked the edge
Of one of many circles.

X   At the sight of the blackbirds
Flying in a green light,
Even the bawds of euphony
Would cry out sharply.

XI   He rode over Connecticut
In a glass coach.
Once, a fear pierced him,
In that he mistook
The shadow of his equipage
For blackbirds.

XII   The river is moving.
The blackbird must be flying.

XIII   It was evening all afternoon.
It was snowing
And it was going to snow.
The blackbird sat
In the cedar-limbs.

WALLACE STEVENS

1 What new insights have you gained from this poem?

2 Using this poem as a pattern, analyze one of the following subjects: love, wolves, home, idols.

3 Write an essay in which you philosophize about the treatment of young people in today's society.

Plaque

A plaque is a notice that is placed for the public to read in a spot that marks or commemorates a significant event. The message is written in a terse, abbreviated style.

1 This plaque is a parody. What is being parodied?

2 Choose a public building in your area that is named after a person. Write a plaque for that building commemorating the person.

3 You are being honoured by the placing of a plaque. Report the event, including the message on the plaque and the crowd's reaction to the event.

4 Create a plaque to mark the arrival on Venus of an international space team.

"...Golly...that has to be the biggest roadside historical sign I've ever seen...!"

Plot

A plot is a plan of action. The writer arranges the events in the story in a pattern that organizes the details so that the reader can remember, and appreciate, the story.

1 This is a plot outline. What must the writer add before it becomes a story?

2 Select one of the strands in this plot and make it into a short story.

3 A plot usually has four elements: introduction, rising action, climax, and conclusion. Work in teams of four. Each team creates a short story based on the computer outline. Each team member writes one element of the plot, choosing any one strand. Then, as a group, create the story from these elements.

4 As a class, create a Mystery Story Pocket Computer.

The Science Fiction
Horror Movie Pocket Computer

Gahan Wilson

25. Create your own S.F. Pocket Computer.

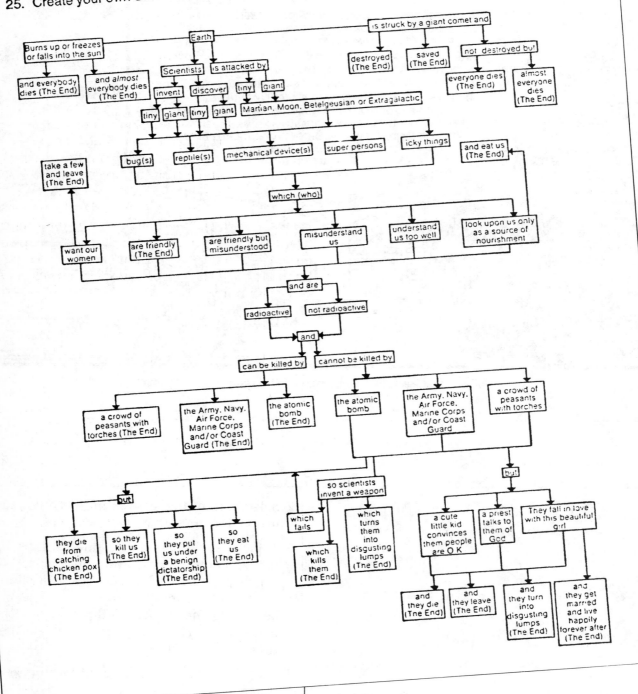

Prayer

Prayer is a form through which people can express their thoughts, their sense of wonder, and their need for help.

The prayer of the monkey

Dear God,
why have You made me so ugly?
With this ridiculous face,
grimaces seem asked for!
Shall I always be
the clown of Your creation?
Oh, who will lift this melancholy from my heart?
Could You not, one day,
let someone take me seriously,
Lord?

Amen

CARMEN BERNOS DE GASZTOLD

Gloria

glory be to the dark to the spark in the dark to
the light of the spark in the dark of the eye

glory be to the farthest star the nearest star to the
moon and the sun and the sea

glory be to the rippled sea the waving sea to the
foaming wildly windy sea to the smooth sea
and the solid sea to the mirror sea of the stars we
see of the moon & the sun & the sky

glory be to the deepest parts of the green blue
gray blue purple sea

glory be to the land to the place where we stand,
the rock, the ridge, the mesa plain, the desert
terrain, the mountain range caves hollows farms
meadows canyons quarries to the snow & the
rain on the mountain range to hail & ice &
thunder to the wind in the sky to the wind on
the plain above the earth & under

glory be to the air to cabbage & pear to pine &
cauliflower to cucumber beet tomato sweet peas
vines & beds & bower zucchini grapes moss fern
lakes & ponds of water lilies, lily of the valley,
lily of the day, morning glory moon glory
sunflower string bean, marsh reed sea weed dill
weed wheat weed watermelon muskmelon
orangemint grape fruit lime parsely sage & lemon
stawberry gooseberry blackberry grass maple
leaf oak leaf cherry leek & linden leaf willow
weep lettuce chives & thyme & turnip onion
garlic carrot plum spinach rice peach pepper tea
rosemary winter savory summer squash & okra
poppy daisy rose watercress posy tarragon mum
and pompon

glory be to the sun

glory be to the rain to the moon and stars and
snow to the night and the day and the milky
way to the wholly holy rainbow.

1 What is the purpose of these prayers?

2 Write a prayer similar to ''The Prayer of the Monkey'' but for another ''ridiculous'' animal.

3 Write another prayer, similar to ''Gloria,'' using the opening line ''Glory be.'' In the prayer, name the joys in your life.

Proclamation

A proclamation is an official announcement, the purpose of which is to set in motion an act of government.

To prevent all persons . . .

AN ACT TO PREVENT ALL PERSONS FROM TEACHING SLAVES TO READ OR WRITE, THE USE OF FIGURES EXCEPTED.

Whereas the teaching of slaves to read and write, has a tendency to excite dissatisfaction in their minds, and to produce insurrection and rebellion, to the manifest injury of the citizens of this State: Therefore,

Be it enacted by the General Assembly of the State of North Carolina, and it is hereby enacted by the authority of the same, That any free person, who shall hereafter teach, or attempt to teach, any slave within the State to read or write, the use of figures excepted, or shall give or sell to such slave or slaves any books or pamphlets, shall be liable to indictment in any court of record in this State having jurisdiction thereof, and upon conviction, shall, at the discretion of the court, if a white man or woman, be fined not less than one hundred dollars, nor more than two hundred dollars, or imprisoned; and if a free person of color, shall be fined, imprisoned, or whipped, at the discretion of the court, not exceeding thirty nine lashes, nor less than twenty lashes.

II. *Be it further enacted,* That if any slave shall hereafter teach, or attempt to teach, any other slave to read or write, the use of figures excepted, he or she may be carried before any justice of the peace, and on conviction thereof, shall be sentenced to receive thirty nine lashes on his or her bare back.

III. *Be it further enacted,* That the judges of the Superior Courts and the justices of the County Courts shall give this act in charge to the grand juries of their respective counties.

To the Queen's Faithful Subjects

In a time of profound peace, while every one was quietly following his occupations, feeling secure under the protection of our laws, a band of rebels, instigated by a few malignant and disloyal men, has had the wickedness and audacity to assemble with arms, and to attack and murder the Queen's subjects on the highway — to burn and destroy their property — to rob the public mails — to threaten to plunder the banks — and to fire the city of Toronto.

Brave and loyal people of Upper Canada, we have been long suffering from the acts and endeavours of concealed traitors, but this is the first time that rebellion has dared to show itself openly in the land, in the absence of invasion by any foreign enemy.

Let every man do his duty now, and it will be the last time that we or our children shall see our lives or properties endangered, or the authority of our gracious Queen insulted by such treacherous and ungrateful men, Militia-men of Upper Canada, no country has ever shown a finer example of loyalty and spirit than you have given upon this sudden call of duty. Young and old of all ranks are flocking to the standard of their country. What has taken place will enable our Queen to know her friends from her enemies — a public enemy is never so dangerous as a concealed traitor: and now my friends let us complete well what is begun — let us not return to our rest until treason and traitors are revealed to the light of day, and rendered harmless throughout the land.

Be vigilant, patient, and active — leave punishment to the laws — our first object is, to arrest and secure all those who have been guilty of rebellion, murder, and robbery; and to aid us in this, a reward is hereby offered of One Thousand Pounds, to any one who will apprehend, and deliver up to justice, William Lyon Mackenzie; and Five Hundred Pounds to any one who will apprehend and deliver up to justice, David Gibson, or Samuel Lount, or Jesse Loyd, or Silas Fletcher; and the same reward and free pardon will be given to any of their accomplices who will render this public service, except he or they will have committed, in his own person, the crime of murder or arson.

And all, but the leaders above-named, who have been seduced to join in this unnatural rebellion, are hereby called to return to their duty to their Sovereign — to obey the laws — and to live henceforward as good and faithful subjects — and they will find the government of their Queen as indulgent as it is just.

GOD SAVE THE QUEEN

1 Who would be affected by each of these proclamations?

2 If the slaves' leaders had had power, what proclamations might they have made in response to the selection "To prevent all persons . . ."?

3 Write a satire on the proclamation "To the Queen's Faithful Subjects." Make modern rebels the subject.

4 Create a class proclamation stating your rights in today's world.

Profile

A profile is a short biography of an interesting person. In the profile, the writer selects significant events and aspects of the subject's life in order to present a full, but brief, portrait.

Jean Little

For Jean Little, a Canadian writer of prize-winning novels for young people, books have always been her window on the world. And reading has always been Jean's chief delight, even though she was born blind and has regained only limited vision over the years.

Fortunately, to help her through her early struggles with reading, and to nurture a love of books, Jean had patient and persuasive parents who took sole responsibility for her early education while they worked as physicians in the mission field. She counts herself fortunate also to have always had living in the Little household an endless company of relatives who have indulged her passion for being read to. And, last, there have been "my friends the librarians, always glad to see me, ever ready with a welcome—despite the mud and snow I tracked in on my daily pilgrimages, despite my clatter and chatter, and despite the book I left out in the thunderstorm, the book the dog ate, the books I lost.

Nor do I remember them ever saying 'Shush,' 'Don't,' or 'Stop.' But rather, 'What did you think of that story?' they'd stop to ask. And I knew they really *wanted* to know because they did something grown-ups didn't often do: they listened. Books were important to them and so was I important, too, because I was one of the people for whom books were written."

It was because of her poor vision that Jean's father presented her with a typewriter of her own. This occurred when, at the outbreak of the Second World War, the Little family finally returned home from Taiwan—where Jean had been born January 2, 1932—and settled in Guelph, Ontario, Canada. Soon, Jean was being encouraged to take after-school typing lessons. These were a torment of pain and humiliation but they brought about their own rewards when she found herself the published author of a collection of poems before reaching her middle teens. "I remember the day I'd been trying to get Dad's attention while he was reading—offering to sing for him, or dance, or something. He seemed totally without interest; so I went away and created a poem, something I'd never tried before. When I returned, Dad threw down his newspaper: 'A poem!' He snatched it out of my hand. 'Let me see it!'" And Jean, who craved nothing more than attention, got it so fast that, there and then, she was launched on a lifelong vocation which has encompassed some dozen children's books that have been translated into Dutch, German, Danish, Japanese, and Russian, and that have won such recognition as Junior Literary Guild Awards, the Canada Council Children's Literature Award, and the Vicky Metcalf

Award for excellence in a body of work that is inspirational to Canadian youth.

Jean Little writes children's books because children's books are chiefly what she reads. She reads them because, for the most part, they are among the few books that still rejoice in life, still pulse with awe and wonder at its miracle, and still communicate a sense of growth and hope and love. It is in this spirit that she writes, to celebrate life and at the same time to move children "to see themselves and their fellows in a fresh light; lend them different eyes to look through; give them a chance to practice the complex art of living as, vicariously, they experience courage, defeat, hope, laughter and love; help them discover the pain and the wonder which will be theirs as they join in the human adventure."

. . . Nowadays, children learning to cope with physical or mental handicaps are central to the themes of many children's books. Many of Jean's books have been in the vanguard of this relatively recent movement, dealing forthrightly but sensitively with such problems as cerebral palsy (*Mine for Keeps*), mental retardation (*Take Wing*), and partial sightedness and blindness (*From Anna* and its sequel, *Listen for the Singing*), in a way that makes such differences "natural and comprehensible" to the young reader. In other novels she explores the lives of children facing psychological handicaps or problems—lying (*One to Grow On*), being a shy and withdrawn only child (*Look Through My Window*), or just social and ethnic difference (*Kate*). Jean Little's characters may have the same handicaps at the end of a book as they do at the beginning, but there is this difference: they have grappled with and conquered the real disabilities—fear, for example (*Stand in the Wind*), or resentment (*Spring Begins in March*), or self-centredness (*Home from Far*), or self-pity and resignation (*Listen for the Singing*). For ultimately, that is the real thrust of Jean Little's novels—recognizing and mastering the enemy within rather than tilting at the one without.

Writing does not come easily to Jean. "You wouldn't believe what people say to me: 'Your books are so sweet . . . sweet little stories and, yes, all kinds of fun. It must be nice to have the words just come bubling out,' a teacher told me not long ago. Bubbling out." The truth is quite otherwise: there is the pain of simply getting started each morning; there is the self-discipline of making writing "a routine of every day of every week of every month";

and there is the most awesome part of the struggle, the launching of the novel—setting the scene, delineating the characters, and priming the plot, so that all elements of the novel are set in motion. This secondary world she has created is what Jean now sets about exploring and recording—tentatively, painfully, curiously. Later the pace changes once again as all thing work their way toward closure, and Jean cannot write fast enough to keep up with the gathering climax and resolution. "Then, all of a sudden, that company of book characters we've been entertaining all these months, maybe years, that we've been learning with during work hours, that we've been conversing with and about at mealtimes, they've gone. Just like that." The wrench of parting is real as the finished manuscript is sent on its way; in time it is eased by the glow of anticipation at sharing a new book with another audience.

Keeping in intimate touch with that audience—the children, their needs, their aspirations, their interests, their problems—is the most important part of Jean Little's job when she is not actually working. Although she has no family of her own, she is close to her several nieces and nephews as well as the many young friends whom she makes through her work in the church, the schools, and the community. She keeps abreast of the field of children's books, and teaches about it throughout North America. She maintains a thriving correspondence with children in places as widely separate as Trieste and Tokyo. . . . An ancedote that she tells about one of those letters captures the essence of Jean Little's writing and her readership's response to it:

I get many letters from children whose teachers have said, "Boys and girls, today you are each going to write to an Author." Once in a long while I get a real letter, a letter written laboriously by one child who has something he or she wants to tell me. One small girl wrote, "Dear Miss Little, You'd think Sally was me." That was what I had been trying to tell her.

MEGUIDO ZOLA

1 Where might this profile have been published?

2 Write the biographical blurb that would appear on the jacket of Jean Little's newest novel. (You are limited to 75 words.)

3 A time capsule is to be buried under the cornerstone of a new building. In the capsule will be a record of our times, including profiles of important people. Write one of these profiles.

4 Interview someone in your school in order to gather information for a profile of that person that will appear in the school yearbook. (For example, consider the custodian, the nurse, or a secretary.)

Prologue

A prologue is an introduction to a play or novel. It establishes a mood, and it helps the audience or reader to understand what is to follow.

Runaways

Conjure the sound of a siren in your brain
the loud wail
its loneliness
the feeling of danger.
What is the siren inside of you?
Who would lock you up?
What are your prisons?
When you make a play about Runaways
you visit very dark rooms in your brain.

We discovered that fantasy saves us —
you can teach yourself to dream.
Out of a pile of paper towels
we made dolls, drums
even spaghetti and meatballs.
We made cousins out of empty shoes
boyfriends and girlfriends out of pillows.
Our parents became the elegant
photographs of antique furniture.
And we believed ourselves totally
as any loners would.

When you make a play about Runaways
you must consider that everyone is hopeful
looking for a family
whether it is a religious organization
a sports team, a street gang
a business office
or a theater group.
Everyone seems to need protection,
some mapped-out answers,
love
or what pretends to be love.
Or what pretends to be love.

Be careful.

ELIZABETH SWADOS

1 What is this play going to be about?

2 Add two more verses to this prologue.

3 This play was created during six months of rehearsals by the young actors from their personal experiences. Write a character sketch of one of these actors that will appear in the program for the play.

A psalm is a song of praise. It is a lyrical, joyful tribute to life.

Psalm 121

The safety of the godly, who trust in God's protection.
A Song of degrees.

I WILL lift up mine eyes unto the hills, from whence cometh my help

2 My help *cometh* from the LORD, which made heaven and earth.

3 He will not suffer thy foot to be moved: he that keepeth thee will not slumber.

4 Behold, he that keepeth Is'rael shall neither slumber nor sleep.

5 The LORD *is* thy keeper: the LORD *is* thy shade upon thy right hand.

6 The sun shall not smite thee by day, nor the moon by night.

7 The LORD shall preserve thee from all evil: he shall preserve thy soul.

8 The LORD shall preserve thy going out and thy coming in from this time forth, and even for evermore.

HOLY BIBLE

Psalm of Those who Go Forth before Daylight

The policeman buys shoes slow and careful; the teamster buys gloves slow and careful; they take care of their feet and hands; they live on their feet and hands.

The milkman never argues; he works alone and no one speaks to him; the city is asleep when he is on the job; he puts a bottle on six hundred porches and calls it a day's work; he climbs two hundred wooden stairways; two horses are company for him; he never argues.

The rolling-mill men and sheet-steel men are brothers of cinders; they empty cinders out of their shoes after the day's work; they ask their wives to fix burnt holes in the knees of their trousers; their necks and ears are covered with a smut; they scour their necks and ears; they are brothers of cinders.

CARL SANDBURG

1 Who were the singers of these psalms?

2 Re-create ''Psalm 121'' as a free-verse poem.

3 Who are today's ''brothers and sisters of cinders'' of those mentioned in ''Psalm of Those who Go Forth before Daylight''? Write a psalm celebrating these people's worth.

Question and Answer

Youth Hot Line

How to win trust

Dear Dr. Cotter:

I would like to know how to win the trust of parents. I have a boyfriend who respects me and would not go further than a kiss if I would not let him.

My parents think I am too young for a steady boyfriend because I might get myself into trouble. He is 15 and I am 14. We don't date alone but always go double or with a group. I've tried talking to my parents but they think I'm too young to understand what they mean.

ANSWER: If you are old enough to write as sensible a letter as this, then you are old enough to know, not only about the possibility of pregnancy, but also that your emotions could get the better of you. Your relationship sounds very good.

How can your parents come to trust you? Perhaps they should realize that a girl of 14 today can be much wiser about personal relationships than a 14-year-old girl of thirty-five years ago.

GRAHAM COTTER

Meddlesome mother

Dear Mr. Vichert:

My boyfriend and I are 16 and we love each other very much. His mother is constantly phoning me and telling me that I can't see her son anymore or she'll do something to me. She says that I'm not the proper girl for her son and that he's too young to be going steady.

We've tried to sit down and talk to his mother to let her know our feelings, but it always turns out to be a one-sided conversation with us doing the listening. What can we do?

ANSWER: You and your boyfriend have tried to solve your problem in a mature and responsible way. Now it is up to your boyfriend. He has to decide what degree of independence is possible for him and to what extent his mother will respect his decisions.

I would hope that his mother would be able to recognize the maturity with which the two of you are handling your relationship and become more supportive.

BRUCE VICHERT

Dear Answer Man

Dear Answer Man
I have heard there are people who eat money. Is this true? *Concerned*

Dear Concerned
You are probably thinking of Cyrus "Piggybank" Wilson, the millionaire, who made a practice of swallowing seventy-five cents (two quarters, two dimes and a nickel) each Thursday of his adult life. How he came to this no-one really knows. A story has it that when he was a boy he would have his allowance stolen by bullies, and so devised this scheme of swallowing what he did not want to lose. In 1963 "Piggy" choked to death on a fifty-cent piece, leaving $364 million in his will and $1.25 in his belly — partially disproving that you can't take it with you.

MAX HOWARD

What is white?

White is a dove
And lily of the valley
And a puddle of milk
Spilled in an alley
A ship's sail
A kite's tail
A wedding veil
Hailstones and
Halibut bones
And some people's
Telephones.
The hottest and most blinding light
Is white.
And breath is white
When you blow it out on a frosty night.
White is the shining absence of all color
Then absence is white
Out of touch
Out of sight.
White is marshmallow
And vanilla ice cream
And the part you can't remember
In a dream.
White is the sound
Of a light foot walking
White is a pair of
Whispers talking.
White is the beautiful
Broken lace
Of snowflakes falling
On your face.
You can smell white
In a country room
Toward the end of May
In the cherry blossom.

MARY O'NEILL

Reply to the Question:

"How Can You Become a Poet?"

take the leaf of a tree
trace its exact shape
the outside edges
and inner lines

memorize the way it is fastened to the twig
(and how the twig arches from the branch)
how it springs forth in April
how it is panoplied in July

by late August
crumple it in your hand
so that you smell its end-of-summer sadness

chew its woody stem

listen to its autumn rattle

watch as it atomizes in the November air

then in winter
when there is no leaf left

invent one

EVE MERRIAM

1 Why is each of these questions being asked?

2 Write an answer to the young person who is asking how to win trust.

3 You are the "Answer Man." Create another "strange" question, then answer it.

4 Using "What is White?" as a pattern, write a poetic definition in answer to the question "What is black?"

5 Create the rules that answer the question "How do you stop people from becoming poets?"

113

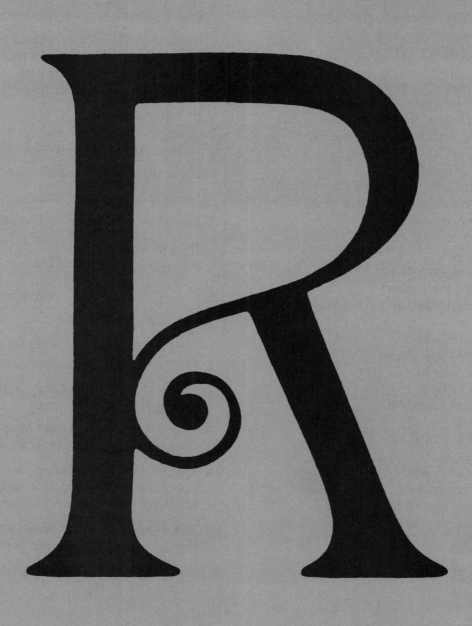

Reportage is the reporting of first-hand observations of newsworthy events.

One Beat with a Bar Ends Gorilla Thriller

HUDDERSFIELD, England (Reuter) — Suddenly the gorilla lurched forward, bent apart the cage bars and lunged at the fairground audience.

An alert spectator grabbed an iron bar and crashed it down on the gorilla's head. Unfortunately, Mike Towell, a regular member of the fair's house of horror, was under the gorilla skin.

Police now want to question the would-be hero, who was last seen running from the tent pursued by Towell, blood streaming from a head wound which needed six stitches.

The Bull Moose

Down from the purple mist of trees on the
    mountain,
lurching through forests of white spruce and
    cedar,
stumbling through tamarack swamps,
came the bull moose
to be stopped at last by a pole-fenced pasture.

Too tired to turn or, perhaps, aware
there was no place left to go, he stood with the
    cattle.
They, scenting the musk of death, seeing his
    great head
like the ritual mask of blood god, moved to the
    other end of
the field, and waited.

The neighbours heard of it, and by afternoon
cars lined the road. The children teased him
with alder switches and he gazed at them
like an old, tolerant collie. The woman asked
if he could have escaped from a Fair.
The oldest man in the parish remembered seeing
a gelded moose yoked with an ox for plowing.
The young men snickered and tried to pour beer
down his throat, while their girl friends took
    their pictures.

And the bull moose let them stroke his tick-
    ravaged flanks,
let them pry open his jaws with bottles, let a
    giggling girl
plant a little purple cap
of thistles on his head.
When the wardens came, everyone agreed it was
    a shame
to shoot anything so shaggy and cuddlesome.
He looked like the kind of pet
women put to bed with their sons.

So they held their fire. But just as the sun
    dropped in the river
the bull moose gathered his strength
like a scaffolded king, straightened and lifted his
    horns
so that even the wardens backed away as they
    raised their rifles.

When he roared, people ran to their cars. All the
    young men
leaned on their automobile horns as he toppled.

ALDEN NOWLAN

1 What makes these events newsworthy?

2 Write the interview that the reporter would have had with the would-be helper mentioned in "One Beat with a Bar Ends Gorilla Thriller."

3 Write the editorial that might have followed the account described in "The Bull Moose."

A requiem is a solemn chant, performed to commemorate a death. The requiem is serious in tone, for it represents people's feelings about their loss.

Requiem for a River

"So we diverted the river," he said,
showing blueprints
and maps
and geological surveys.
"It'll go in this canal now."

The Rio Blanco River starts in a glacier
up the white-capped Andes.
It has run through a green valley
for three million years,
maybe more.

Now in this year
when the Rio Blanco copper mine
at 12 000 feet altitude
gets underway,
the river has to go.

Pick it up,
Move it over —
Anything is possible.
Don't stand in the way
of progress,
And a 90-million-dollar mine.
"We concreted the dam," Bert said.

Thanks.

KIM WILLIAMS

Lost in France, Jo's Requiem

He had the ploughman's strength
in the grasp of his hand;
He could see a crow
three miles away,
and the trout beneath the stone.
He could hear the green oats growing,
and the south-west wind making rain.
He could hear the wheel upon the hill
When it left the level road.
He could make a gate, and dig a pit,
and plough as straight as stone can fall.
And he is dead.

ERNEST RHYS

1 What are the two poets commemorating in these requiems?

2 There were many Canadian soldiers lost in France during World War Two. Create the requiem honouring the Unknown Canadian Soldier.

3 Using "Requiem for a River" as a pattern, write another environmental requiem for something that is about to be lost because of civilization's progress.

4 Write a letter to the producer of a television show that you feel represents life in a silly or negative way. What will you say is being lost to society?

Review

A review serves several purposes: it announces to the public that a film or book is available, briefly describes the work, discusses its technical qualities, and compares it with other, similar works. The purpose of a review is to help people decide whether to read, see, or listen to what is being reviewed.

MAJOR, KEVIN, *Hold Fast*. 170p. CIP. Delacorte. Mar. 1980. CSm $8.95. ISBN 0-440-03506-6. LC 79-17544. *Gr 6-10*—Michael is only 14 when his parents die in an auto crash and he is sent to live with his uncle's family in a suburban area far from his Newfoundland fishing village. His uncle turns out to be a cruel bully, and when his country dialect brings taunts from students in his new school and he is suspended for fighting, Michael and his cousin, Curtis, run off to a remote National Park. There, they survive for several days on wild rabbits, "holding fast" to the land like the native seaweed. Author Major is a specialist in Newfoundland lore and literature and this fine, first novel, which is very well written and constructed (it has won the Canadian Children's Librarians' Book of the Year Award) includes brief, interesting sketches of life in a Newfoundland village and a great deal of local language usage, which might confuse some readers. Michael is strong and likable and by the time he returns to his beloved village we know him very well and are not at all surprised when everything works out for the better. *Robert Unsworth*

A School Responds to "What Color Is The Wind?"

From the teachers If schooling is a process of growth in mind and spirit, then this film belongs in every classroom. It combines lovely photography with a rare and beautiful message of the human spirit. No young person should be deprived of the opportunity to join in blind three-year-old Lee Rubenstein's discovery of the world — a happy world shared with his twin brother, Jeff, and his parents. We become more human by becoming part of their lives and loves, by realizing that daily living can be precious, and is not to be wasted. Our thanks to Allan Grant, the filmmaker, for his beautiful ode to life. It electrified all of us at Covena High School here in California, had us talking to one other about its beauty, joyousness, and courageous outlook. We want everyone to see this film. — Don Kenyon and John Ewing, English teachers.

From the students
The worst handicap that Lee will meet will be how people treat him, not the inability to see. Everyone around the boy will value his or her sight much more because of his influence, while he will appreciate his other senses as most other people never will. — Dana Roskey

● When a boy is that small or young, he must really miss his eyes. Children like to investigate, learn things, touch things and play. Jeff, his brother, gives him eyes, helps him in so many areas. He helps him play and understand how other kids play. — Tammy Harkness

● You do not need to see something in order to be something. What color is the wind? The wind is any color; this to one person and that to another. — Chris Ender

● The film has a special way of conveying the joy of a trial. How happy the boy is, and how simple his problem is to himself. — Mike McCasland

● The film really "opened my eyes." It made me conscious of the things we see that a blind person can't. — Ken Wong

1 Which of these reviews is most effective?
2 Write a review of one of your school textbooks. The review is to be published in a teachers' professional journal.
3 The film reviews presented here are highly personal and emotional. Write a review of a film or television show that has moved you emotionally.
4 Choose a character from a novel. Write the monologue that the character would give about his or her situation in life.

Rules

Rules are a means of conducting and ordering society. They establish standards that must be obeyed so that society can run smoothly. Rules can be written or unwritten.

Rules of Conduct

Each teacher will bring a bucket of water and a scuttle of coal for the day's session . . . will fill lamps, clean chimneys and trim wicks. Men teachers may take one evening each week for courting purposes, or two evenings if they go to church regularly. After school, teachers should spend the remaining time reading the Bible or other good books. Women teachers who marry or engage in other unseemly conduct will be dismissed. Every teacher should lay aside a goodly sum so that he will not become a burden on society. Any teacher who smokes, uses liquor, frequents pool or public halls, or gets shaved in a barber shop, will give good reason to suspect his worth, intentions, integrity, and honesty. The teacher who performs his labour faithfully and without fault for five years will be given an increase of 25 cents per week in his pay if the School Board approves.

MANITOBA, 1880

My Rules

If you want to marry me, here's what you'll have
    to do
You must learn how to make a perfect chicken
    dumpling stew
And you must sew my holey socks and you must
    soothe my troubled mind
And develop the knack for scratching my back
And keep my shoes spotlessly shined
And while I rest you must rake up the leaves
And when it is hailing and snowing
You must shovel the walk, and be still when I
    talk
And — hey, where are you going??

SHEL SILVERSTEIN

1 Who is making these sets of rules?

2 Create a national set of rules for parents, standardizing the raising of children.

3 In "My Rules," the speaker's original rules failed; therefore he must amend them. Write his new rules for finding and keeping love.

4 Write an editorial entitled "We are over-ruled and over-regulated."

Satire

Satire uses humour to point out weaknesses in society. The writer makes fun of human endeavours in an attempt to demonstrate how they might be changed and improved.

Two Ways to Wake a Sleepwalker

I

Not too abruptly, now,
any shock may start up
something none of us can
finish. Maybe a little
tug on his pajama sleeve
will serve. No sudden noises
please. I read somewhere
it's bad to bring them
out of it too suddenly.

He doesn't know what's
going on or where he's
headed. Give him some
direction or he'll simply
drift in mystery from
room to room. He doesn't
really see what lies
ahead of him. Best to
guide him back to bed.

When morning comes, he
won't remember anything.
We can joke about it
then. Best without a doubt
to keep him half asleep
and let him dream it out.

II

Kick him. Nothing like
a sudden jolt to bring him
out of that unearthly
lethargy. Can't stand
to see a human being
anything but wide awake —
much less this dumb body
going through such empty
mindless motions.
                    Slap

his stupid face until
he realizes who and
where he is. I bet he'll
thank us when he learns we
wouldn't stand for stupor.
Whole damn world is watching
every move we make, so
do it quick. There's
got to be some pain.

Kick him hard so he'll
remember who it was
that brought him howling
out of it and taught him
what it really means
to really be awake.

EDWARD LUEDERS

120

Alfred G. Graebner Memorial High School Handbook

1. WELCOME TO ALFRED G. GRAEBNER MEMORIAL HIGH SCHOOL! TO RETURNING STUDENTS, WE ARE GLAD TO SEE YOU BACK AGAIN. TO NEW FRESHMEN, WE HOPE YOU WILL SOON FEEL AT HOME HERE. THIS HELPFUL HANDBOOK WILL SERVE AS YOUR GUIDE TO AGGMHS AND PROVIDE YOU WITH MUCH NEEDED INFORMATION ABOUT YOUR SCHOOL, ITS FACILITIES, AND THE RULES AND REGULATIONS BY WHICH WE ALL ABIDE.

2. ANY STUDENT MAY SUBMIT WORK FOR PUBLICATION IN THE LITERARY MAGAZINE "TAPROOTS," WHICH IS THE VEHICLE FOR CREATIVE EXPRESSION OPEN TO ALL WHO SEEK A LITERARY OUTLET.

3. THE ONLY LEGAL EXCUSES FOR ABSENCE OR TARDINESS ALLOWED UNDER THE STATE EDUCATION LAW ARE SICKNESS, DEATH IN THE FAMILY OR RELIGIOUS OBSERVANCE.

4. ELECTIONS FOR CLASS OFFICERS WILL BE HELD EVERY NOVEMBER. ALL STUDENTS SHOULD TAKE PART IN THEIR STUDENT GOVERNMENT, EITHER BY RUNNING FOR OFFICE, OR BY VOTING FOR THE CANDIDATE OF THEIR CHOICE. REMEMBER! STUDENT GOVERNMENT IS YOUR GOVERNMENT!

ELLEN CONFORD

1 What aspects of society are being satirized in these selections?

2 Following the style of "Alfred G. Graebner Memorial High School Handbook," write a set of satirical rules that should be posted on the wall of every fast-food restaurant.

3 "Two ways to wake a sleepwalker" is a comparison poem: one half presents a valid attitude, while the other satirizes an invalid attitude. Using this poem as a pattern, write a poem entitled "Two Ways to Give a Friend Advice."

Scenario

A scenario is the working script for a film or television program. Included in a scenario are the dialogue spoken by the actors, the setting, the movement, the camera positions, and the lighting.

Singin' in the Rain

Grauman's Chinese Theater — Hollywood
The scene is Hollywood in 1927, at the peak of the silent-movie era just prior to the introduction of sound pictures. It is the night of a big premiere. First we see huge beams of light searching the sky from big searchlights placed around the theater. We see the front of the Chinese Theater and enormous crowds along Hollywood Boulevard, and from the clothes of the people, we see that we are in the late 1920's. The marquee reads: PREMIERE TONIGHT—BIGGEST PICTURE OF 1927—DON LOCKWOOD AND LINA LAMONT IN "THE ROYAL RASCAL."

*A couple of kids have climbed a palm tree and are looking at the sign. The police are holding back surging crowds which are pressing against ropes forming an aisle from the street to the entrance to the theater. The aisle is covered with red carpeting. A girl is clutching a fan magazine (*Screen Digest*—25¢) on the cover of which we see a picture of two movie stars and the heading "Lockwood and Lamont — Reel Life or Re-al Life Romance?" About three-quarters of the way up the aisle to the theater is a large, old-fashioned microphone, and to either side high poles topped with the flaring horns of an early public-address system. At the microphone stands Dora Bailey, a smartly dressed, matronly woman, a leading film columnist, who is addressing the crowd. She bears an unmistakable resemblance in both looks and voice to Louella Parsons.*

DORA (*highly excited; in an overecstatic, gushy voice*): This is Dora Bailey, ladies and gentlemen — talking to you from the front of the Chinese Theater in Hollywood. What a night, ladies and gentlemen — what a night! Every star in Hollywood's heaven is here to make Monumental Pictures' premiere of *The Royal Rascal* the outstanding event of 1927. Everyone is breathlessly awaiting the arrival of Lina Lamont and Don Lockwood. Oh —
A shriek goes up from the crowd as a limousine pulls up in front of the theater.
DORA (*continuing*): Look who's arriving now. It's that famous "Zip Girl" of the screen, the darling of the flapper set, Zelda Zanders —
Zelda Zanders, a flaming "It Girl" type, shimmies up the

aisle accompanied by a very old doddering man in evening clothes.

— and her new red-hot pash — J. Cumberland Spendrill III, that well-known eligible bachelor.

CROWD (*rising and screaming*): Ohhhhhhhhhh!

A MAN IN THE CROWD (*beside himself*): Zelda! Ohhhh! Zelda!

Zelda poses with Spendrill III as photographers cluster around and light bulbs flash. They turn and go into the theater.

DORA: Zelda's had so much unhappiness. I hope this time it's really love.

Another limousine has pulled up and an exaggeratedly exotic woman of the Jetta Goudal! - Nita Naldi variety steps out, wrapped in a long black cape. She is accompanied by a suave, be-moustached type in top hat and tails.

DORA: And look who's just arrived. It's that exotic star Olga Mara and her new husband, the Baron de la Bouvet de la Toulon.

CROWD: Ohhhhhhhhhh!

As Olga and the Baron proceed grandly up to the theater, she lets the cape open, and drags it slinkily along the ground, while photographers' bulbs flash.

DORA: They've been married two months already, but still as happy as newlyweds.

Another car has pulled up.

DORA: Well, well, well, it's —

There is an expectant hush. Then a man gets out of the car, starts up the aisle, dressed in evening clothes, boyish and anonymous-looking. It is Cosmo Brown. The crowd that has begun to lean forward expectantly is puzzled and disappointed.

CROWD (*sighing*): Ohhhhh!

DORA (*continuing*): Cosmo Brown.

Cosmo looks around, smiling embarrassedly, then stops next to Dora as she goes on.

Cosmo is Don Lockwood's best friend. He plays the piano on the set for Don and Lina to get them into those romantic moods.

Suddenly she is terribly excited.

Oh, oh, folks, this is it! This is it!

Two motorcycle policemen come roaring past the front of the theater and stop, followed by a super-limousine that does likewise. A liveried doorman steps forward to open the door as the crowd cheers in expectation, and photographers rush forward to capture the great moment.

DORA (*transported*): The stars of tonight's picture, those romantic lovers of the screen — Don Lockwood and Lina Lamont!

Policemen are pushing photographers back, and as the blur of bodies clears away, we see Don Lockwood and Lina Lamont standing in front of the limousine door. They are a truly dazzling sight, and the crowd goes insane, welling and surging against the ropes. Don is a dashingly handsome, buoyantly athletic-looking young man. Over his evening suit he is wearing a white camel-hair coat with a fold-over belt with matching soft-brimmed white hat,

and is sporting a million-watt white-toothed smile. Lina is the epitome of classic patrician beauty, regal, elegant, and slightly aloof, a vision of devastating loveliness. They are both waving at the crowd, and Don throws kisses in their direction, to a response of deafening cheers. The screaming crowd is held back. One woman faints against the arms of two policemen. Lina and Don walk forward, still waving, and step up to greet Dora, with Cosmo still standing beside her, and they all cluster around the microphone. Don shakes hands with Cosmo.

DORA: Ladies and gentlemen, when you look at this gorgeous couple, it's no wonder they're a household name all over the world, like bacon and eggs — Lockwood and Lamont!

From now on we see that Don does all the public-appearance talking for the two of them, while Lina just smiles, with a certain false graciousness, covering her annoyance.

DORA (*gushing*): Don, you can tell me confidentially, are these rumors true that wedding bells are soon to ring for you and Lina?

DON: Well, Lina and I have no statement to make at the present time. We're just good friends.

DORA: You've come a long way together, Don. Won't you tell us how it all happened?

DON: Well, Lina and I have made a number of pictures together.

DORA: Oh, no, no, Don. I want your story from the beginning.

DON (*looking around self-effacingly*): Oh, Dora, not in front of all these people.

CROWD (*as one*): Yes!

DORA: But, Don, the story of your success is an inspiration to young people all over the world. Please!

This interview is to be considered as a number, during which, in ironic contrast to Don's voice giving a fabricated biography, we see what really took place in Don's life and career.

DON: Well, to begin with, any story of my career would have to include my lifelong friend, Cosmo Brown. We were kids together — grew up together — worked together —

DORA: Yes?

DON (*with hammy, false humility*): Well, Dora — I've had one motto which I've always lived by — Dignity — always Dignity. This was instilled in me by Mum and Dad from the very beginning. They sent me to the best schools — including dancing school. That's where I first met — Cosmo. And with him I used to perform for all Mum and Dad's society friends.

A Disreputable-looking Poolroom

Don, as a small boy in ragged clothes, is tap-dancing as tough poolroom characters throw him an occasional penny. Cosmo as a small boy is playing the harmonica.

DON'S VOICE: They used to make such a fuss over me.

A burly-looking saloon keeper grabs the boys as they bend

to pick up the coins and carries them through the swinging doors.

DON'S VOICE: Then if I was very good, I was allowed to accompany Mum and Dad to the theater. They brought me up on Shaw, Molière, the finest of the classics —

The Front of an Old Nickelodeon Theater
There is a poster of a girl in African safari outfit in the clutches of a gorilla; the poster reads: ''The Dangers of Drucilla — with Esme Gray — 12th Episode.'' We see the boys sneak past the ticket taker and go in.

In Front of the Chinese Theater
DON: To this we added rigorous musical training — at the Conservatory of Fine Arts.

A Dingy Café
Don and Cosmo, now grown up, still in ragged clothes, are playing respectively a fiddle and a piano — in a band.

DON'S VOICE: We then rounded out our apprenticeship in the arts at the most exclusive dramatics academy. *A sign saying* AMATEUR NIGHT.

BETTY COMDEN AND ADOLPH GREEN

1 How is this scenario different from the script of a play?

2 One of the selections in this book is about to be filmed. Create the scenario to be used by a television producer. (An example of a suitable selection is ''Two Friends'' by David Ignatow.)

3 Turn this selection into a script for use as a stage play.

4 Write a brief research essay entitled ''The New Hollywood Musicals.''

Science fiction

Science fiction is a form of fantasy based on scientific facts. The author, using this knowledge as a basis, creates adventures in other dimensions of time and space.

Men Are Different

I'm an archaeologist, and Men are my business. Just the same, I wonder if we'll ever find out about Men — I mean *really* find out what made Men different from us Robots — by digging around on the dead planets. You see, I lived with a Man once, and I know it isn't as simple as they told us back in school.

We have a few records, of course, and Robots like me are filling in some of the gaps, but I think now that we aren't really getting anywhere. We know, or at least the historians say we know, that Men came from a planet called Earth. We know, too, that they rode out bravely from star to star; and wherever they stopped, they left colonies — Men, Robots, and sometimes both — against their return. But they never came back.

Those were the shining days of the world. But are we so old now? Men had a bright flame — the old word is ''divine,'' I think — that flung them far across the night skies, and we have lost the strands of the web they wove.

Our scientists tell us that Men were very much like us — and the skeleton of a Man is, to be sure, almost the same as the skeleton of a Robot, except that it's made of some calcium compound instead of titanium. Just the same, there are other differences.

It was on my last field trip, to one of the inner planets, that I met the Man. He must have been the last Man in this system, and he'd forgotten how to talk — he'd been alone so long. Once he learned our language we got along fine together, and I planned to bring him back with me. Something happened to him, though.

One day, for no reason at all, he complained of the heat. I checked his temperature and decided that his thermostat circuits were shot. I had a kit of field spares with me, and he was obviously out of order, so I went to work. I turned him off without any trouble. I pushed the needle into his neck to operate the cut-off switch, and he stopped moving, just like a Robot. But when I opened him up he wasn't the same inside. And when I put him back together I couldn't get him running again. Then he sort of weathered away — and by the time I was ready to come home, about a year later, there was nothing left of him but bones. Yes, Men are indeed different.

ALAN BLOCH

The Animal That Drank Up Sound

1

One day across the lake where echoes come now
an animal that needed sound came down. He gazed
enormously, and instead of making any, he took
away from, sound: the lake and all the land
went dumb. A fish that jumped went back like a
    knife,
and the water died. In all the wilderness around
    he
drained the rustle from the leaves into the
    mountainside
and folded a quilt over the rocks, getting ready
to store everything the place had known; he
    buried —
thousands of autumns deep — the noise that
    used to come there.

Then that animal wandered on and began to
    drink
the sound out of all the valleys — the croak of
    toads,
and all the little shiny noise grass blades make.
He drank till winter, and then looked out one
    night
at the stilled places guaranteed around by frozen
peaks and held in the shallow pools of starlight.
It was finally tall and still, and he stopped on the
    highest
ridge, just where the cold sky fell away
like a perpetual curve, and from there he walked
    on silently,
and began to starve.

When the moon drifted over that night the whole
    world lay
just like the moon, shining back that still
silver, and the moon saw its own animal dead
on the snow, its dark absorbent paws and quiet
muzzle, and thick, velvet, deep fur.

2

After the animal that drank sound died, the
    world
lay still and cold for months, and the moon
    yearned
and explored, letting its dead light float down
the west walls of canyons and then climb its
    delighted
soundless way up the east side. The moon
owned the earth its animal had faithfully
    explored.
The sun disregarded the life it used to warm.

But on the north side of a mountain, deep in
    some rocks
a cricket slept. It had been hiding when that
    animal
passed, and as spring came again this cricket
    waited,
afraid to crawl out into the heavy stillness.
Think how deep the cricket felt, lost there
in such a silence — the grass, the leaves, the
    water,
the stilled animals all depending on such a little
thing. But softly it tried — 'Cricket!' — and back
    like a river
from that one act flowed the kind of world we
    know,
first whisperings, then moves in the grass and
    leaves;
the water splashed, and a big night bird
    screamed.

It all returned, our precious world with its life
    and sound,
where sometimes loud over the hill the moon,
wild again, looks for its animal to roam, still,
down out of the hills, any time.
But somewhere a cricket waits.

It listens now, and practises at night.

WILLIAM STAFFORD

1 What statements are these two writers making about life?

2 Write the report that the archaeologist in ''Men are Different'' would submit to explain his failure to bring back a human specimen.

3 Write the free-verse poem, based on ''The Animal that Drank up Sound,'' in which the cricket waits, dreading the return of ''the moon's animal.''

4 In a time warp, you have been transported back to the age of the Stone People. They have decided to sacrifice you in order to ensure that the sun returns after the eclipse. Write the speech in which you convince them that the eclipse is only temporary and that the sun will return, naturally.

A playwright tells a story through the speech of the characters in his or her play. The actors use the script to help the audience understand the action, meaning, and mood of the play.

The Black and White

The FIRST OLD WOMAN *is sitting at a milk bar table. Small.*
A SECOND OLD WOMAN *approaches. Tall. She is carrying two bowls of soup, which are covered by two plates, on each of which is a slice of bread. She puts the bowls down on the table carefully.*

SECOND: You see that one come up and speak to me at the counter?
She takes the bread plates off the bowls, takes two spoons from her pocket, and places the bowls, plates and spoons.

FIRST: You got the bread, then?

SECOND: I didn't know how I was going to carry it. In the end I put the plates on top of the soup.

FIRST: I like a bit of bread with my soup.
They begin the soup. Pause.

SECOND: Did you see that one come up and speak to me at the counter?

FIRST: Who?

SECOND: Comes up to me, he says, hullo, he says, what's the time by your clock? Bloody liberty. I was just standing there getting your soup.

FIRST: It's tomato soup.

SECOND: What's the time by your clock? he says.

FIRST: I bet you answered him back.

SECOND: I told him all right. Go on, I said, why don't you get back into your scraghole, I said, clear off out of it before I call a copper.
Pause.

FIRST: I not long got here.

SECOND: Did you get the all-night bus?

FIRST: I got the all-night bus straight here.

SECOND: Where from?

FIRST: Marble Arch.

SECOND: Which one?

FIRST: The two-nine-four, that takes me all the way to Fleet Street.

SECOND: So does the two-nine-one *(Pause.)* I see you talking to two strangers as I come in. You want to stop talking to strangers, old piece of boot like you, you mind who you talk to.

FIRST: I wasn't talking to any strangers.
Pause. The FIRST OLD WOMAN *follows the progress of a bus through the window.*
That's another all-night bus gone down. *(Pause.)* Going up the other way. Fulham way. *(Pause.)* That was a two-nine-seven. *(Pause.)* I've never been up that way. *(Pause.)* I've been down to Liverpool Street.

SECOND: That's up the other way.

FIRST: I don't fancy going down there, down Fulham way, and all up there.

SECOND: Uh-uh.

FIRST: I've never fancied that direction much.
Pause.

SECOND: How's your bread?
Pause.

FIRST: Eh?

SECOND: Your bread.

FIRST: All right. How's yours?
Pause.

SECOND: They don't charge for the bread if you have soup.

FIRST: They do if you have tea.

SECOND: If you have tea they do. *(Pause.)* You talk to strangers they'll take you in. Mind my word. Coppers'll take you in.

FIRST: I don't talk to strangers.

SECOND: They took me away in the wagon once.

FIRST: They didn't keep you though.

SECOND: They didn't keep me, but that was only because they took a fancy to me. They took a fancy to me when they got me in the wagon.

FIRST: Do you think they'd take a fancy to me?

SECOND: I wouldn't back on it.
The FIRST OLD WOMAN *gazes out of the window.*

FIRST: You can see what goes on from this top table. *(Pause.)* It's better than going down to that place on the embankment, anyway.

SECOND: Yes, there's not too much noise.

FIRST: There's always a bit of noise.

SECOND: Yes, there's always a bit of life.
Pause.

FIRST: They'll be closing down soon to give it a scrub-round.

SECOND: There's a wind out.
Pause.

FIRST: I wouldn't mind staying.

SECOND: They won't let you.

FIRST: I know. *(Pause.)* Still, they only close hour and half, don't they? *(Pause.)* It's not long. *(Pause.)* You can go along, then come back.

SECOND: I'm going. I'm not coming back.

FIRST: When it's light I come back. Have my tea.

SECOND: I'm going. I'm going up to the Garden.

FIRST: I'm not going down there. *(Pause.)* I'm going up to Waterloo Bridge.
SECOND: You'll just about see the last two-nine-six come up over the river.
FIRST: I'll just catch a look of it. Time I get up there. *Pause.* It don't look like an all-night bus in daylight, do it?

HAROLD PINTER

1 What do you know about these characters?

2 Using the style of ordinary conversation, as in "The Black and White," write the script of two strangers in a hospital room. The script must reveal their true characters.

3 Choose a newspaper story and retell the incident using only dialogue.

Sermon

A sermon is a speech telling people how to conduct their lives.

Whispers

(It is the breath of the ancestors)

Listen more often to things than to beings
    Hear the fire's voice,
    Hear the voice of water.
    Hear, in the wind, the sobbing of the trees.
It is the breath of the ancestors.

The dead are not gone forever
They are in the paling shadows,
They are in the darkening shadows.
    The dead are not beneath the ground,
    They are in the rustling tree,
    In the murmuring wood,
    The flowing water,
    The still water,
    In the lonely place, in the crowd;
    The dead are never dead.

Listen more often to things than to beings.
    Hear the fire's voice.
    Hear the voice of water.
    In the wind hear the sobbing of the trees.
    It is the breath of the ancestors.
    They are not gone
    They are not beneath the ground
    They are not dead.

The dead are not gone forever.
    They are in a woman's breast,
    A child's cry, a glowing ember.
    The dead are not beneath the earth,
    They are in the flickering fire,
    In the weeping plant, the groaning rock,
    The wooded place, the home.
    The dead are never dead.

Listen more often to things than to beings
    Hear the fire's voice,
    Hear the voice of water.
    Hear, in the wind, the sobbing of the trees.
    It is the breath of the ancestors.

BIRAGO DIOP

Translated by SAMUEL ALLEN

1 What is this speaker's message?

2 Using "Whispers" as a pattern, write a sermon that you would give to a high-school graduating class to persuade them to approach life in a positive way.

3 You are the Wise One speaking to your people in the year 2500. The youth have refused to accept the wisdom of the ages. In your speech, you warn them of their fate if they continue to disregard the past.

A short story is a work of fiction. It deals with a single incident or event, and it must begin, be developed, and end, all in a limited space.

The Mask

It was old now, and its shriveled inside pinched and scratched his stinging face. But as he glanced in the full-length mirror, he could see its outside still peacefully smiling. Ever since he put it on it had been smiling exactly that way.

When he had arrived at the party and someone had handed him the mask, he had politely declined, saying he didn't care for it. But someone in a huge grinning mask said that if he didn't put it on people might not think he was enjoying the party. And if they thought him unhappy they might even ask him to leave.

At first the mask seemed tolerable. It felt good, looked real, and made him feel like one of the crowd. Once behind it, it didn't matter whether he liked the party or anyone at the party. Nobody would know.

But as the party progressed, he noticed all the masks beginning to look more and more alike: smiling, happy, self-satisfied. He glanced in the mirror; even his own mask was beginning to look that way. Worse still, those who hadn't accepted masks looked as though they were enjoying themselves more than those who had.

Suddenly he was afraid. What if his mask should slip down in an unguarded moment? What if everyone should discover that behind the mask he wasn't really having fun at all?

As the huge grinning mask had said, they might ask him to leave. And the irony of the whole thing was that the person assigned to dismiss unhappy partygoers was also wearing a mask, a person who — behind his own mask — might be even more miserable than he.

He stared at his peacefully smiling reflection in the mirror. It was nauseating. Behind him some masks were whispering among themselves. A masked voice was saying they should try harder to spread more masks around — there would be greater security against discovery that way. But the voice sounded pinched.

Perhaps they wouldn't dismiss him after all. Perhaps, if he took it off, he could start a trend. Perhaps others would follow and they could laugh and be happy again.

He had worn his mask too long already, and it was getting old. Its drying, shrinking inside chafed and pinched his face. Suddenly it lost all meaning. It hadn't changed the real him at all. It was a sham, a facade, a mockery. He would tear it off and throw it away!

He reached for it, no longer caring what anyone else thought or said or did. He despised it. He wanted his face to be *his* — not some grinning mask's. His fingers searched for the string, for the edge — but the string was gone, and he couldn't find where the mask left off and his skin began.

Looking in the mirror, he clutched frantically at the shriveled mold and pulled until his whole face stung and burned in pain. A scream escaped his smiling lips. The mask had grown onto his face.

MAX PHILLIPS

The Castaway

The man on the raft had only hope to keep him alive now. The bones showed through his thin face. An endless moan escaped his trembling mouth. His eyes were bright with fever. He had been clinging to life for more than a month now on this wretched collection of planks.

All at once a new sound reached his enfeebled brain: a buzzing noise imagined in his delirium no doubt. But it wasn't — it really was a helicopter approaching slowly, flying over the raft. Saved! He was saved! The castaway danced about clumsily.

In the meantime a rope-ladder had been lowered from the helicopter. A man dressed in rags, his emaciated face overgrown with a coarse beard, was pushed brutally on to the top rungs.

The helicopter turned away and disappeared.

Now there were two castaways on the raft.

ROLAND TOPOR

Appointment in Samarra

DEATH SPEAKS: There was a merchant in Baghdad who sent his servant to market to buy provisions and in a little while the servant came back, white and trembling, and said, Master, just now when I was in the market-place I was jostled by a woman in the crowd and when I turned I saw it was Death that jostled me. She looked at me and made a threatening gesture; now, lend me your horse, and I will ride away from this city and avoid my fate. I will go to Samarra and there Death will not find me. The merchant lent him his horse, and the servant mounted it, and he dug his spurs in its flanks and as fast as the horse could gallop he went. Then the merchant went down to the market-place and he saw me standing in the crowd and he came to me and said, Why did you make a threatening gesture to my servant when you saw him this morning?

That was not a threatening gesture, I said, it was only a start of surprise. I was astonished to see him in Baghdad, for I had an appointment with him tonight in Samarra.

W. SOMERSET MAUGHAM

1 Choose one of these short stories, and prepare a plot outline for it. Compare the outlines prepared for the three stories.

2 Write a short story, based on an incident in which the smiling face of the character in "The Mask" leads him to grief.

3 Write the sequel to "Appointment in Samarra." It is to be called "Death in Samarra."

4 Write the proclamation that was issued ordering the second castaway to the raft in the story "The Castaway."

Soliloquy

A soliloquy is a speech in a play that is spoken by a character as if he or she were alone and thinking aloud.

Werewolf

As lights come up Bernard is discovered sitting on a ledge, his hands positioned as if on a steering wheel, his eyes look straight ahead.

WEREWOLF (BERNARD). One night, driving home to evening cocktails, I was suddenly struck through the windshield by the rays of the full moon. (*He rises.*) And I grew body hair, pointed ears — cloven hooves, and a tail. And I thought, "At last! It's the real me!" And with fear secretly mingled with delight I arrived home — where my wife said, "Your dinner's cold — and stop looking at me in that accusing way!" And my son said, "All the other daddies are good at fixing things, you've got fingers like claws!" And my little girl said, "Why do I have to have the only father on the block who's different?" So I ate them all up. (*He takes a napkin from his pocket and wipes his mouth with it.*) Werewolves really shouldn't marry. (*Loud knocking is heard coming from door.*)

JULES FEIFFER

1 Why did the author decide that it was important that Bernard give this soliloquy?

2 Write the soliloquy spoken by Bernard's mother describing her son's true nature.

3 Write a soliloquy in which you describe your fears of the future.

Song

A song is a composition written to be sung. It usually has a rhythmic pattern, and it often creates a particular mood.

Life in a Prairie Shack

1 Oh, a life in a prairie shack, when the rain begins to pour!
Drip, drip, it comes through the roof, and some comes through the door.
The tenderfoot curses his fate and faintly mutters, 'Ah!
This blooming country's a fraud, and I want to go home to my Maw!'

CHORUS:
'Maw! Maw! I want to go home to my Maw!
This blooming country's a fraud, and I want to go home to my Maw!'

2 Oh, he saddled his fiery cayuse, determined to flourish around;
The critter began to buck, and threw him off on the ground,
And as he picked himself up he was heard to mutter, 'Ah!
This blooming country's a fraud, and I want to go home to my Maw!'

3 Oh, he tried to light a fire at twenty degrees below.
He made a lick at a stick and amputated his toe,
And as he crawled to his shack he was heard to mutter, 'Ah!
This blooming country's a fraud, and I want to go home to my Maw!'

4 Now all you tenderfeet list, before you go too far:
If you haven't a government sit, you'd better stay where you are,
And if you take my advice, then you will not mutter, 'Ah!
This blooming country's a fraud, and I want to go home to my Maw!'

Collected by EDITH FOWKE

The First Night of Christmas

Come to me the first night of Christmas
I shall give you one fish,
All upon one dish.

Come to me the second night of Christmas
I shall give you two chickens, one fish,
All upon one dish.

Come to me the third night of Christmas
I shall give you three cakes, two chickens, one fish,
All upon one dish.

Come to me the fourth night of Christmas
I shall give you four slaughtered sheep, three cakes, two chickens, one fish,
All upon one dish.

Come to me the fifth night of Christmas
I shall give you five fat ones, four slaughtered sheep, three cakes, two chickens, one fish,
All upon one dish.

Come to me the sixth night of Christmas
I shall give you a sow with six pigs, five fat ones, four slaughtered sheep, three cakes, two chickens, one fish,
All upon one dish.

Come to me the seventh night of Christmas
I shall give you seven salted fry for cooking, a sow with six pigs, five fat ones, four slaughtered sheep, three cakes, two chickens, one fish,
All upon one dish.

Come to me the eighth night of Christmas
I shall give you eight oxen with grain fields, seven salted fry for cooking, a sow with six pigs, five fat ones, four slaughtered sheep, three cakes, two chickens, one fish,
All upon one dish.

Come to me the ninth night of Christmas
I shall give you nine straight-horned goats, eight oxen with grain fields, seven salted fry for cooking, a sow with six pigs, five fat ones, four slaughtered sheep, three cakes, two chickens, one fish,
All upon one dish.

Come to me the tenth night of Christmas
I shall give you ten early-bearing cows, nine
straight-horned goats, eight oxen with grain
fields, seven salted fry for cooking, a sow with
six pigs, five fat ones, four slaughtered sheep,
three cakes, two chickens, one fish,
All upon one dish.

Come to me the eleventh night of Christmas
I shall give you eleven trusses of hay, ten early-
bearing cows, nine straight-horned goats, eight
oxen with grain fields, seven salted fry for
cooking, a sow with six pigs, five fat ones,
four slaughtered sheep, three cakes, two
chickens, one fish,
All upon one dish.

Collected by EDITH FOWKE

1 These two songs are folk songs. What are the clues to support this statement?

2 Write the lyrics for a folk song that describes and comments upon your own difficult situations in a humorous way.

3 Using the pattern of "The First Night of Christmas," write the lyrics for the Christmas song for the year 2001.

4 Choose two songs that you like. Write an essay in which you discuss the point "Are songs poems, or do they need the tune to be complete?"

Sonnet

A sonnet is a lyric poem of 14 lines that follow a definite rhyming scheme. There are two types of sonnets: the Italian (with end rhymes abba abba cde cde) and the English (with end rhymes abab cdcd efef gg). The first eight lines describe the poet's feelings, and the last six lines comment on those feelings.

The Old Bridge at Florence

Taddeo Gaddi built me. I am old,
   Five centuries old. I plant my foot of stone
   Upon the Arno, as St. Michael's own
   Was planted on the dragon. Fold by fold
Beneath me as it struggles, I behold
   Its glistening scales. Twice hath it overthrown
   My kindred and companions. Me alone
   It moveth not, but is by me controlled.
I can remember when the Medici
   Were driven from Florence; longer still ago
   The final wars of Ghibelline and Guelf.
Florence adorns me with her jewelry;
   And when I think that Michael Angelo
   Hath leaned on me, I glory in myself.

HENRY WADSWORTH LONGFELLOW

Death Be not Proud

Death be not proud, though some have called
   thee
Mighty and dreadful, for thou art not so;
For those whom thou think'st thou dost
   overthrow
Die not, poor death, nor yet canst thou kill me.
From rest and sleep, which but thy pictures be,
Much pleasure; then from thee much more must
   flow,
And soonest our best men with thee do go,
Rest of their bones, and soul's delivery.
Thou art slave to fate, chance, kings, and
   desperate men,
And dost with poison, war, and sickness dwell;
And poppy or charms can make us sleep as well,
And better than thy stroke; why swell'st thou
   then?
One short sleep past, we wake eternally,
And death shall be no more; death, thou shalt
   die.

JOHN DONNE

1 What are the rhyme schemes of these sonnets?

2 Celebrate a monument in your community by writing a sonnet to it, using the pattern of "The Old Bridge at Florence."

3 Write a sonnet entitled "Live life proudly," using the pattern of "Death Be not Proud."

4 Re-write one of these sonnets as a haiku.

Speech

A speech is a formal type of oral presentation. It is given to an audience, which has gathered to hear the speaker.

Touch the Earth

We have come to ask the agent that we be sent home to our own country in the mountains. My people were raised there, in a land of pines and clear, cold rivers. There, we were always healthy, for there was meat enough for all. We were happy there until the Great Father's soldiers brought us here. Now, in the year that we have been in this southern country, many of us have died. This is not a good place for us — there is too much heat and dust and not enough food. We wish to return to our home in the mountains. If you have not the power to give us permission to go back there, let some of us go on to Washington and tell them there how it is; or do you write to Washington and get permission for us to go back North? . . . We cannot stay another year; we want to go now. Before another year has passed, we may all be dead, and there will be none of us left to travel north.

Collected by T. C. McLUHAN

Family

"Apes," I began, "I am not an orator. I am a common ape, like you. I say what I think. I have been a captive for all of my life, but this does not mean that I am less an ape than any other. I have lived most of my life as a subject for research. Some apes think that research apes consider themselves superior to other apes, but that is because they may not have been associated with research projects before. Apes are apes, wherever they may be. Most are kind; some are not. Most are bright and lively; some are not. Most are generous; some are selfish. Apes are apes. And I am an ape.

"So know that I am speaking ape to ape when I tell you what I must tell you."

There was a stirring. Myrtle closed her eyes. She was crying.

"The humans here have a plan. It is a heavy plan. It is about their future.

"They think that one day in their future, humans will be able to be made up of parts that other humans will put together. The humans think that in the future, copulation will not be a factor associated with creating lives. They think they will be able to assemble themselves and take themselves apart according to their needs.

"We — you and I — will help them, they think."

A great stirring then occurred.

"I want no part of this experiment," I said.

A shrieking began, and grew louder and louder. Humans in great numbers came to the gymnasium. Apes did the unspeakably rude thing they sometimes do when they want to show their contempt for humans. The humans hate it, to be hit with what we throw. It is a dirty and brutish act, but not an inappropriate one when the occasion warrants. The apes felt this to be an appropriate occasion. The humans left in haste. We apes were left alone.

"What next, Sasha?" one of the apes said.

"We must leave this place," I said.

JOHN DONOVAN

1 What are the occasions on which these speeches were given?

2 You are the agent in the selection "Touch the Earth." Write the speech that you will give to these people on this occasion.

3 Write the transcript of the conversation that takes place around the table the morning after the events in "Family," as the scientists discover that the apes have disappeared.

4 Supposing chickens could vote in elections. Write the politician's campaign speech given to the chickens.

> Stream of consciousness writing is the uninterrupted flow of the thoughts and images that occur in a writer's mind while writing. The writer records personal thoughts, memories, emotions, and associations as they pass through his or her consciousness.

The Hôtel La Salle

Hard pelting snow, like the skins of small arctic land-mammals. Walking. The fish, still animate, that I found lying in a foreign bed of whiteness. Crystals forming on its flesh, but the fish breathed yet. Its eyes rolled as much as they could, bewildered to observe me. I bent down, cold, to touch this fish and the pain that came to my ungloved hand was fantastic. In shock, having jumped back, I realized that the eye-movements made by the fish had been to warn me from making contact. I was not the first to attempt to caress this sorry-looking creature. In a quiet turmoil I continued on my way. Like the time I found that moist larva-like entity between the sheets of some old poetry I was storing beneath my bed — it had no visible legs or eyes, just stiff damp wings. I freed it but it did not fly. It must have been the early stages of a butterfly using my papers as a cocoon — perhaps a unique physical manifestation of my words. I seem to grasp the significance of this symbol then it slips away. I'm stray again. The day I was walking hand in hand with myself down the suburban paveways singing, for anyone caring to hear, a violent ditty. When I looked back there was real smoke rising from my footprints. The dark guts of night fell on me at once. Or the time I awoke, wearing my finest of garments, to find myself lying stomach-down on a public sidewalk — quite a stupor that was in the noonday sun. Once I helped some men tear down the wall of a flat to discover, in common amazement, the taxidermed body of a woman having tea. Sometimes in the cold I'd wrap sheets of leopard-skin wallpaper around myself and be mistaken for the Hôtel La Salle, where the elevators are but jocular windpipes of a dead thing greater than ourselves; where damp meals burst into flames on your dinner-plate; where the bellboys will escort you in privacy down a hallway, or perhaps a stairwell, then — when assured that the inhabitants of the building have left the two of you in solitude — begin screaming and clutching at your clothing with teeth bared in a frenzied smile (refusing, nevertheless, your gracious tip); where monkeys hang motionlessly from the draped ceiling of your room — so much so that you don't notice them until almost asleep, then, in a brief grotesque convulsion, you catch sight of their unmalicious but very perturbing stares; where lovely young women with dark hair and thick passionate wrists string themselves out in slumber on the hall floors — when you approach and bow yourself over one in closer proximity, however, you realize with a sweating heart that these women are not at all earthly, not natural in any godly sense of the word at all; where your bed-sheets quiver once or twice each night without your prompting them; where sonic booms are as common as a candleflame, and as welcome as a morning's tactile wake-up call; where operations are performed for free; the Hôtel La Salle, where once I spent a honeymoon alone.

STEWART WRIGHT

1 How does the author connect these random images to form a story?

2 Write a segment of a novel in which the reader learns what is going on in the mind of one character through the stream-of-consciousness style.

3 Write the stream-of-consciousness thoughts that would have occurred to one of the following at a moment of crisis: a racing-car driver, a rock star, a gymnast, a marathon swimmer, a surgeon.

Synopsis

A synopsis is a summary of the main points of a longer piece of writing.

TV Guide

JANUARY 17, 1975

bery. Hadley: Chris Alcaide. Hewitt: Robert Knapp. Laurie: Pat Barr. Hadley: John Milford.

11:20 ③ ⑩ ⑪ ⑫ ⑬ **NEWS**
⑥ **SPORTS**
⑨ **NIGHT BEAT NEWS—Martineau**

11:30 ② ⑧ **JOHNNY CARSON**
Scheduled guests include singer Ian Whitcomb. Ed McMahon. (90 min.)
④ **MERV GRIFFIN**
⑤ **FINAL EDITION**
⑥ **SIMPLY CHARLOTTE**
⑦ **MOVIE—Crime Drama**
"Murder Once Removed." (1971) Made-for-TV suspense yarn with Barbara Bain as a partner in a deadly romantic triangle. Ron: John Forsythe. Frank: Richard Kiley. (90 min.)
⑩ **UNTOUCHABLES** BW
Bugs Moran, in hiding since the St. Valentine's Day massacre, is visited by Eddie O'Gara (Mike Connors)—who claims he can put Bugs back on top of the rackets. Ness: Robert Stack. Bugs: Robert J. Wilke. Vince: Sean McClory. (60 min.)
⑪ **LARRY SOLWAY**
Photographer John de Visser.
⑬ **MOVIE—Drama** BW
"Death Party." (German; 1964) German singers encounter hostility when their tour bus breaks down in postwar Yugoslavia. Herbert: Goetz George. Seja: Milana Dravic. Otmar: Gerlach Fiedler. Friedrich: Hans Nielsen. (2 hrs.)
⑰ **ABC NEWS—Smith/Reasoner**
Captioned for the hearing-impaired.

11:35 ㉙ **MOVIE—Comedy** BW
"A Woman of Distinction." (1950) A dignified college dean (Rosalind

Friday
EVENING

Russell) and a staid British professor (Ray Milland) are reluctantly thrown together for a series of farcial situations. Teddy: Janis Carter. Mark: Edmund Gwenn. Paul: Francis Lederer. (2 hrs.)

11:45 ⑩ **MOVIE—Adventure**
"Billion Dollar Brain." (English; 1967) Finland's winter scenery highlights this complex yarn featuring reluctant spy Harry Palmer (Michael Caine). Filmed in Helsinki and Latvia. Newbegin: Karl Malden. Anya: Francoise Dorleac.

11:50 ⑫ **MOVIE—Adventure**
"The Far Country." (1955) Action during a cattle drive to Alaska. James Stewart, Walter Brennan, John McIntire. Renee: Corinne Calvet. Ronda: Ruth Roman. Gannon: Jay C. Flippen. Ives: Steve Brodie. (1 hr., 55 min.)

12:00 ③ **MOVIE—Drama**
"The Dark at the Top of the Stairs." (1960) Fine adaptation of William Inge's play about small-town life in the 1920s. Robert Preston, Dorothy McGuire, Eve Arden, Angela Lansbury, Shirley Knight, Richard Eyer, Lee Kinsolving. (2 hrs., 25 min.)
⑤ **DON KIRSHNER'S ROCK CONCERT**
Martha Reeves, Leo Kottke, Larry Raspberry and the Highsteppers, and Kansas are guests. Songs include "Power of Love" (Martha), "Hear the Wind Howl" (Leo). (1 hr., 20 min.)
⑥ **MOVIE—Mystery**
"Fragment of Fear." (English; 1970) David Hemmings as an ex-drug addict investigating his aunt's murder in

TV GUIDE 14-105

"The Moustache"; #1050/23; March 17, 1952.

When Ricky grows a moustache for a TV role, Lucy takes reciprocal action. She doesn't like kissing a man with a moustache and insists he shave it off at once. Having a little fun with her, Ricky hints he might keep it for good, even after the TV stint. This really annoys Lucy, so she borrows a fake beard from Fred and attaches it to her face with what appears to be spirit gum. When Ricky comes home, she kisses him — to give him a taste of his own medicine. He is amused by her joke, but asks her to remove the false whiskers. She can't. They've been glued on with Bulldog Cement, not mere glue, and Lucy fears she'll have to be a bearded lady for life. But what really makes her distraught is that Ricky is bringing home a talent scout for whom she naturally wants to audition. Her valiant efforts to hide the white mane behind the veil of a harem-girl outfit fail, and Ricky loses out on the TV job.

BART ANDREWS

Capsule History of Canada

1891. Invention of basketball by Dr. James Naismith, native of Almonte, Ont. An oustanding athlete at McGill University, Naismith was a staff member of the International YMCA Training School at Springfield, Mass., when he was asked to create a game that would fill the gap between football and baseball seasons; now a world-wide game, basketball is still played by Dr. Naismith's 13 basic rules.

1892. Governor-General Stanley donated hockey's most famous trophy. Originally, the Stanley Cup was about 25cm high; with base panels added to accommodate engraving of winner's names, it is now over one metre high. Lord Stanley was a keen hockey fan, made up a team at Rideau Hall from among his eight sons.

1896. Gold discovered in Klondyke by George Carmack and two Indians. Skookum Jim and Tagish Charlie, on tip from prospector Robert Henderson. Stampede started the following year, when word reached the outside. In two years Dawson was a city of 25 000. In eight years $100 000 000 worth of gold was recovered by hand methods. Henderson got back too late to stake gold claims, received only a small pension as original discoverer.

1897. Canada's first gasoline-driven car built in Sherbrooke, Que., by George Foss, a 20-year-old bicycle repairman. Foss had a ride in an electric automobile in Boston came and built a one-cylinder gasoline car that gave him 12 kilometres to the litre and that he drove for four years before he sold it. Henry Ford was just starting up in Detroit and asked Foss to come in with him, but in his 80s Foss said that if he had become involved in the worries of a big business he never would have lived as long.

1900. An attempt to blow up the Welland Canal lock at Thorold. Three Americans were involved. Two of them set off a charge of dynamite against a lock gate; it was incorrectly placed and opened only a small hole, although it could have drowned thousands. The trio were easily arrested because the third man, who was supposed to arrange the getaway in a fast buggy, dallied in a Niagara Falls saloon.

1901. Mrs. Annie Edson Taylor, a Michigan school teacher, went over Niagara Falls in a wooden barrel with an anvil for ballast. Mrs. Taylor's feat gained her some fame but no money, although she was the first of the four who have survived a deliberate ride over the Falls. Mrs. Taylor's first words when they opened the barrel were, "Nobody ought ever to do that again."

1903. Helping build a railway in northern Ontario, a blacksmith named Fred LaRose threw a hammer at a fox's eyes shining in the dark. He missed the fox but hit the world's richest silver vein, started one of the greatest mining stampedes in history. It founded the city called Cobalt because there was so much cobalt mineral in the silver ore. LaRose sold his claim for $30 000. The Timmins brothers, Noah and Henry, were in the group of buyers, and that started them on their remarkable mining carrer.

Death of Emily Howard Stowe, Canada's first woman doctor. A Toronto school teacher at fifteen, after teaching for ten years she married and decided to become a doctor, but no college here would admit women and she had to study in the U.S. She graduated in 1867, but it was another 13 years before she could convince the men to admit her to practice. Later she helped start the Toronto School of Medicine, for women only.

1904. Nova Scotia moose introduced to Newfoundland as addition to large native caribou herds; have thrived tremendously. Newfoundland's native animals differ from mainland—no snakes, frogs, squirrels, skunks, etc.

Editors of QUICK CANADIAN FACTS

1 Why were these synopses written?

2 Write synopses, suitable for a television guide, for three other television programs.

3 Create a section of the shooting script based on the synopsis of the episode from "Ricky and Lucy."

4 Compose three more interesting entries to go into *Capsule History of Canada.*

A transcript is a record of a conversation. The recording may be done by a writer or by a machine. In a transcript, there is no narration; the reader reads only the words of the speaker or speakers. Transcripts may come from such situations as interviews, trials, or someone's recollections.

Well, You Just Worked, Hard

One sure thing about those days, we sure knew how to work. It wasn't exactly that we called it work, it was more like just part of our lives.

If I'm not mistaken, I couldn't have been more than six when I put my childhood things away, my toys and slingshots and my pets, and the only time I looked at them again, I guess, was when I dug them out again and gave them to my kid brother to play with.

It was the same with girls too, you might say. Yes, the same with my sisters.

Even before five or six, though, we were doing things around the yard, hunting up broody hens and getting them back to the henhouse, and going for the cows with Spot, our collie, and handing my dad things when he was fixing a piece of machinery, oiling it, replacing a part that he'd fixed. He did his own blacksmithing. Everybody did, but not the hard parts. Or in the summer I'd load up my little wagon with two stone mason jars, one of water and one of lemonade, and with sandwiches and cake and cookies I'd go out to the field where the men were working and give them afternoon lunch.

Of course, you never went between the barn and the house but what you didn't pick up a load of poplar wood for the woodbox. If you came in without it you got a glare, and maybe if my mother was in a snarky mood you got a clout on the ear, which you tried to duck and she'd say, "C'mere you," and give you a worse one. Wonder us kids didn't get ear trouble that way. Even if you could only manage a few sticks you brought something. I've seen my two-year-old sister Mary toddling along with one little stick in her arms and getting a pat on the head from my mother.

When I was seven or so, there I was, winter or summer, milking my one cow, and then it got to be two cows and three, until by about nine I was doing a man's job with the cows, milking, carrying the pails to the house, getting the De Laval separator turning.

I've seen me on the summer fallow at 11 years old, hardly big enough then to get the harness on, and me with a four-horse team, and at seven in the morning seeing all the other kids going down the roads to school, where I should have been going except Dad said the field had to be done, and that was that and I did it. I remember there was one kid named Jim Davis who used to go by just like he was a cowboy. On a Shetland pony. I'd ask Dad for a Shetland pony and he always said, "A Shetland pony shouldn't be for children. There's no meaner horse alive. Good only for a cart," he said. "Half the horse bites in this country are from them little critters." At the time if I was big enough to handle harrows and a four-horse team, then maybe I was man enough to handle a Shetland pony, but that's one thing about my father: what he said stood as gospel and that pretty well was that.

I didn't mind it so much. One thing in those days, and maybe still now, you were proud of your strength, proud you could work like a man even though you were just a boy in years. But actually you were a man because by the time you were 13 or so and had the knack for farming, which you would pretty well have, there wasn't much you didn't know around the place.

Transcribed by BARRY BROADFOOT

1 How is a transcript such as this selection different from the accounts given in a history textbook?

2 Work with a partner, one being the interviewer (recording the information), the other being the subject. The year is 2050: the subject recollects his or her childhood.

3 As a class project, create a collage of transcripts that represents the school hall at lunch time. The snippets of conversations must be actual.

4 Write a letter to the editor from the speaker in the selection printed here. The subject of the letter is "Today's children are soft."

Urban tales

The Hook

There was this couple sitting in a car at Lover's Lane near Midland, Ontario. They turned on the radio in time to hear a flash that a mentally insane person had broken out of the Penetang Hospital for the Mentally Insane and that people should be on the look-out for him because he was dangerous. He could be recognized by the hook on his right hand.

The couple talked about this for a little while and the girl asked the guy to take her home because she was a little scared. The guy said that there was nothing to worry about because the man would never be around there where they were. Still the girl insisted on going home. Her boyfriend was annoyed and the car screeched off to take her home. After seeing his girl to the door he started walking back to his car and suddenly saw this hook on the door handle of the passenger side of the car.

BRIAN SMITH, 14, WILLOWDALE, 1973.

Hot Dog!

It seems there was an old lady who had been given a microwave oven by her children. After bathing her dog she put it in the microwave to dry it off. Naturally, when she opened the door the dog was cooked from the inside out.

JAN HAROLD BRUNVAND

Babysitter Mistakes Child for Turkey

This story was told to me by a friend who heard it on the news on the radio a year or so ago. It is a factual account.

There was a girl and she was babysitting. The parents had gone out to a very big party and had left this infant at home with this sixteen-year-old girl. So she was babysitting and they phoned just to see if everything was all right. She said, "Oh, fine. Everything's great. The turkey's in the oven." The mother went, "Oh, okay, fine," and she hung up. Then she looked at her husband and went, "The turkey's in the oven? We didn't have a turkey!" He said, "What's the matter?" So they decided they had better go home and see what was the matter. Maybe there was something wrong with the babysitter.

They excused themselves from the party and went home. So they walked in the house and saw the babysitter sitting in the chair freaking out. She had put the little infant in the oven and had thought it was a turkey.

JENNY NIX, 16, TORONTO, 1973.

1 Although these three tales never happened, what makes them so believable?

2 Write another version of the urban tale "Hot Dog."

3 What urban tales have been passed on to you by your family or friends? Do any of those collected tales have the same origin?

4 Write a short story beginning with, "This is not an urban tale. It actually happened to me."

Valentine

Kidnap Poem

ever been kidnapped
by a poet
if i were a poet
i'd kidnap you
put you in my phrases and meter
you to jones beach
or maybe coney island
or maybe just to my house
lyric you in lilacs
dash you in the rain
blend into the beach
to complement my see
play the lyre for you
ode you with my love song
anything to win you
wrap you in the red Black green
show you off to mama
yeah if i were a poet i'd kid
nap you

NIKKI GIOVANNI

Valentine

Chipmunks jump, and
Greensnakes slither.
Rather burst than
Not be with her.

Bluebirds fight, but
Bears are stronger.
We've got fifty
Years or longer.

Hoptoads hop, but
Hogs are fatter.
Nothing else but
Us can matter.

DONALD HALL

1 To whom are these valentines addressed?

2 The kidnapper's condition for release is that you write a Valentine to the kidnapper. Base your valentine on the "Kidnap Poem."

3 Write another parody based on the "Roses are red" type of valentine.

4 Write an Unvalentine poem to Ming the Merciless.

Verse

Verse is a form of poetry. It is simple in content. Its main quality is its strong rhythm and rhyme.

Street Song

O, I have been walking
with a bag of potato chips,
me and potato chips
munching along,

Walking alone
eating potato chips,
big old potato chips,
crunching along,

walking along
munching potato chips,
me and potato chips
lunching along.

MYRA COHN LIVINGSTON

Umbilical

You can take away my mother,
you can take away my sister,
but don't take away
my little transistor.

I can do without sunshine,
I can do without Spring,
but I can't do without
my ear to that thing.

I can live without water,
in a hole in the ground,
but I can't live without
that sound that sound that sound that sOWnd.

EVE MERRIAM

Hannah Bantry

Hannah Bantry,
In the pantry,
Gnawing at a mutton bone;
How she gnawed it,
How she clawed it,
When she found herself alone.

TRADITIONAL

Last Night, the Night Before

Last night, the night before,
A lemon and a pickle came a-knockin' at my
    door.
When I went down to let them in,
They hit me on the head with a rollin' pin.
This is what they said to me:
    Lady, lady turn around,
    Lady, lady touch the ground,
    Lady, lady show your shoe,
    Lady, lady how old are you?
    1, 2, 3, etc.

TRADITIONAL

1 Are these selections part of the world of poetry?

2 Compose another skipping rhyme similar to "Last Night, the Night Before" that modern children might use.

3 Write a second verse of the old nursery rhyme "Hannah Bantry," exploring her character in more detail.

4 Create another fast-food rhyme to be chanted, as in "Street Song."

5 Write a monologue in which you argue to be allowed to keep your transistor radio.

Western

A Western is a story set in the Old West. Originally, Westerns dealt with the adventurous lives of frontier men and women. Westerns usually follow a simple formula, with stereotypical characters and a predictable plot.

Dust Was the Color of the Sky

ust was the color of the sky.
Dust was the color of the town.

The young sheriff moved toward the railway platform, pausing only to wipe his moist palms on his holsters.

He watched the Union Pacific engine hurtle around the bend and screech to a clanging, hissing stop. Silently, the Dalton boys swung from the train onto the station platform. Suddenly the sheriff found himself staring down the barrels of three shotguns. The street behind him was empty but for the dust.

There was no turning for help.

As his hands crept slowly toward his gun belt he knew he had to say it now or forever hold his peace. A crooked smile played about the corners of his mouth, as he drawled, "Boys, I want you to hear me and hear me good. Just remember, that Xerox is a registered trademark of Xerox Corporation and, as its brand name, should be used only to identify its products and services."

Smile When you Play Them!

1 What elements of the Western are evident in these selections?

2 Choose another common product, and advertise it using another element commonly found in Westerns.

3 Create a safety poster using another stock character found in a typical Western.

4 Write a short research essay entitled "The cowboy: myth or reality?"

Word play

The goal of word play is to manipulate and have fun with language. It includes tongue twisters, riddles, puns, verses, signs, and jokes.

Celebearties

BEARGESS MEREDITH	ROBEART REDFORD
BEARBARA STANWYCK	CLAUDETTE COLBEAR
ALLAN GINSBEARG	INGRID BEARGMAN
P. T. BEARNUM	BEARY GOLDWATER
JAMES THURBEAR	WILBEAR WRIGHT
RICHARD CHAMBEARLIN	BARBEARA STREISAND
VINCE LOMBEARDI	ROBEART FROST
AUBREY BEARDSLEY	CARL SANDBEARG
CHE GUEBEARRA	BEAR ABBIE
CAROL BEARNETT	BEARIO ANDRETTI
DAVID BEARINKLEY	HUCKLEBEARY FINN
BEARY MANILOW	MILTON BEARLE
KATHERINE HEPBEARN	IRVING BEARLIN

PHYLLIS DEMONG

Newfoundland Riddles

Brown I am, and much admired,
Many horses have I tired.
  Tire a horse and weary a man,
  Tell me this riddle if you can.
—A saddle.

I went into the woods and got it;
I sat down to look for it;
The more I looked for it, the less I liked it;
Not being able to find it, I came home with it.
—Thorn in foot.

Collected by ELIZABETH B. GREENLEAF

Autograph Verses

I oughta smile
  I oughta laugh
  But in this book
  I autograph.

Find new friends
  But keep the old,
  One is silver
  The other gold.

Collected by EDITH FOWKE

Old MacDonald Had an Apartment House

Old MacDonald lived in a big apartment house with his wife and their dog. He didn't own the building. Fat Mr. Wrental did. Old MacDonald was its Super.

JUDITH BARRETT *and illustrated by* RON BARRETT

Tongue Twister

You've no need to light a night light
On a light night like tonight,
For a night light's light's a slight light,
And tonight's a night that's light.
When a night's light, like tonight's light,
It is really not quite right
To light night lights with their slight lights
On a light night like tonight.

ANONYMOUS

1 Each of these selections is related to one of the other modes in the book. Name each of the original modes.
2 Write a CATalogue of puns, based on the pattern of "Celebearties".
3 Write some verses for the autograph books of Christopher Columbus, Louis Riel, Marilyn Monroe, and Santa Claus.

X-word

A crossword puzzle involves both fun and skill. The writer of a crossword puzzle must have a wide knowledge of words and how they are used.

Double-Crostic

A. Sit in your _ _ _ _, Tom Grout.
B. They don't play banjos in Hawaii, they play _ _ _ _ _ _ _ _ .
C. Take the _ _ _ down, Fowler. We're not playing volleyball today.
D. 700 _ _ _ _ _ _ _ _ _ _ by 4 equals 2 900. _ _ _ _ _!
E. Don't _ _ _ _ _ , Sarah.
F. But I really don't _ _ _ _ well, Miss Simmons.
G. I _ _ _ _ you she'd find out.
H. His office is crazy. It's all dark and dusty. There are heaps of bones and skulls lying all around. It's like the _ _ _ _ _ _ _ _ _ .
I. You're ikky, Jane Wilcox. I _ _ _ _ you.
J. Name five countries which border the Mediterranean _ _ _ , Mary.
K. Ha. Geez. Look what Sam _ _ _ .
L. President Franklin D. Roosevelt _ _ _ _ on April 12, 1945.
M. Samuel Cohn, what are you hiding under your _ _ _ _?
N. a b c d e f g h _ j k l m n _ p q r s t u v w x y z.
O. Samuel Cohn, _ _ _ _ _ up!
P. _ _ _ _ _ is the opposite of light.

Q. It's not a toad, Miss Simmons, it's a _ _ _ _ .
R. Tom Grout, will I have to _ _ _ _ _ _ _ you to your desk like a horse?
S. My brother told me that once when Miss Simmons was teaching first _ _ _ _ _ a boy sassed her, and she lifted him right up out of his chair and turned him _ _ _ _ _-turvy.
T. Yeah, but I'd still rather have her _ _ _ _ Miss Carter.
U. _ _ _ me! Miss Carter doesn't pinch as hard.
V. Yeah? Then why'd you _ _ _ _ " _ _ !" when she pinched your ear yesterday?
W. _ _ _ is that man or whom is _ _ _ _ man?
X. I'll throw it so it _ _ _ _ _ _ against the blackboard, but I won't throw it at her.
Y. 100 times 100 000 equals _ _ _ _ _ _ _ _ .
Z. All right. Who threw the peanut _ _ _ _ _ _ sandwich?
   I am _ _ _ _ _ _ _ disgusted with all of _ _ _ .
* Hey Bill, I'll _ _ _ _ you to the water fountain.
♥ _ _ _ _ fo fum.

THOMAS AND GAIL ROCKWELL

1 Using the "Double Crostic" parody of a X-word, create another set of clues. Use the theme, The Football Game.

Yarns

A yarn is a kind of humourous folk tale. Yarns are told in everyday speech, and they are usually about wild, impossible happenings, usually involving superhuman qualities.

Buffalo Movers

Well, he said, "When I was livin' with my wife in my young married days, years ago, when there was lots of buffalo on the prairie, we lived in a nice log cabin with spring water just outside the door. My wife asked me to get a pail of water. When I went outside and looked around, I found the cabin was a kilometre from the water. It seemed that the buffalo rubbin' theirself on the corner of the building through the night had moved the cabin a kilometre from the water hole."

ANDREW WRIGHT

Outracing the Chinook

Dave McDougall lived at Morley, which is about 80 kilometres west of Calgary, on the Bow River. He started to town with a team and bobsleigh. He was traveling east. A lot of snow was on the ground when he left his home. On the road he was overtaken by a chinook. (Chinooks always come from the west.) It was a particularly warm chinook, and, fearing that he wouldn't get to town before the snow melted, he whipped up the horses to a gallop. The snow melted so fast that the front runners were on snow but the back runners were in the mud. Try as he might he could not go fast enough to get the back runners out of the mud and up on to the snow.

ALEX R. McTAVISH

Bunyan's Trick

Paul says to me, one time, he says, "We can make a little bit of money now quite easy," and I says, "Yeah? How do we do it?" "Well," he says, "You know where Boyd's big island is on Pigeon Lake. Well," he says, "we'll move that big island 'way down into Gannon's Narrows, and we'll block the channel, and," he says, "then they'll have to pay us twice that much to get it back." I says, "All right," so he says, "What you got to do, catch a lot of those mud turtles — those big snapping mud turtles." So I got about a thousand of them and took them up to old Paul, and he placed them in channels, you know, right all around the island. And they love bananas, mud turtles, so we got a long pole and we kind of hung some bananas on the end of this pole and held them out like that, and they come up and come up and come up to get the bananas, and we knew the way we wanted it to go, you know — south, and they just went right after those bananas, and accordance they did, they were hitched to the big island they had to move it, and they walked right away to Gannon's Narrows with it. Well, we got five thousand dollars for that.

ANONYMOUS

"Yarns" collected by EDITH FOWKE

1 What makes these selections yarns?

2 Using the characters from "Buffalo Movers," tell the yarn about how the settler moved the cabin back to its original spot.

3 Tell the tall tale the children told as to why they were late getting home from berry picking.

4 Tell the yarn Paul Bunyan spun about the time he reversed Niagara Falls.

Zodiac

The zodiac is made up of twelve signs named for the stellar constellations. By charting the signs of the zodiac, astrologists claim to be able to read character and foretell the future.

1 The dictionary defines zodiac as "imaginary" and astrology as a "pseudo-science." Is this horoscope to be read as truth or fiction?

2 Conduct a survey among your friends and relatives in order to determine the accuracy of this brief zodiacal horoscope. Write a report of your findings.

3 Write an essay supporting or attacking astrology.

The Signs of the Zodiac

Aries—The Ram
March 21 to April 19
Quick-tempered, restless and self-willed is Aries.
Girl, if you marry him you will not marry ease.
Fickle but generous, a handsome slob,
He gives the orders and you do the job.

Taurus—The Bull
April 20 to May 19
Both earthy and stubborn is Taurus,
With a tendency also to bore us
    By his total recall
    Of details so small
That he's perfectly prepared to spend a whole
    evening telling us who said what in a
    conversation he had sixty million years
    ago with a rather dull brontosaurus.

Gemini—The Twins
May 20 to June 20
Niminy-piminy
Fidgety Gemini —
He's a bit womany,
    She's a bit he-manny.
Half-knowing, half-guessing,
    Half-feeling, half-thinking,
They're in in a flash and
    They're out in a winking.

Cancer—The Crab
June 21 to July 22
Timid and easily downcast
The gentle Crab adores the past
And cowering from the present's blast
Mourns for her shell before the last.

Leo—The Lion
July 23 to August 21
Hark to Leo's lazy roar!
See the common herd adore!
Why should Leo work to prove
That he's worthy of their love?
Leo's such a natural king
He needn't do a single thing.

Virgo—The Maiden
August 22 to September 22
Early one evening
Just as the Moon was rising
I heard the Maiden singing
    In her clear, chilly voice
"Oh, I'm so witty,
Oh, I'm so pretty,
How can it be that
    I don't get the boys?"

Libra—The Scales
September 23 to October 22
In the House of Scales
Such balance prevails
That if, say, a chair
Is just here, then it's clear
That one must be there
To balance the pair.
And of much the same kind
Is the Libran in mind.
He will balance each plan
As long as he can
(Until sometimes, it's true, it
Is too late to do it.)

Scorpio—The Scorpion
October 23 to November 21
Walk ye humbly! Speak ye low!
Here comes Mr Scorpio!
For one who looks so stern and moral
He's mighty quick to pick a quarrel.

Sagittarius—The Archer
November 22 to December 21
Hurrah, hurrah for Sagittarius!
In action quick, in wit hilarious,
His virtues are so large and various
To number them would only weary us.
A snob, perhaps, but nothing serious . . .
Yes, I myself am Sagittarius!

Capricorn—The Goat
December 22 to January 20
Delightful little babies born
Under the sign of Capricorn
    May well grow up as mighty scholars.
But even if they're mighty fools
They know a thing not taught in schools—
    They know and feel the smell of dollars.

Aquarius—The Water-Bearer
January 21 to February 19
Who sits brooding all alone
    With a time-bomb in his mind?
Who runs to help the crippled crone
    And finds a pathway for the blind?
If these are truly both Aquarius
His age may feel a mite precarious.

Pisces—The Fish
February 20 to March 20
If will were wish
    If dare were dream
These lazy fish
    Would rule the stream.

PETER DICKINSON

Index of Titles and Topics